GW00778124

Personal and Collaborative Leadership

A Handbook

3rd Edition

Éamonn McGuinness

Published by Lead Inside Out Publications
Galway, Ireland

All enquiries to books@leadinsideout.org

Third Edition

ISBN (hard copy): 978-1-9993598-1-2
Distributed by Amazon Books

Cover and interior diagrams illustrated
by Alan Geraghty and Ray Glasheen.

Helpful feedback, reviews and ideas for this third edition generously
provided by Alan Geraghty, Chris Lowney, Grace Windsor, Jonathan
Weisglass, Paul Madden, Seán O'Shea and Simon Gorman.

DEDICATION

This book is gratefully dedicated to the loving memory of Philip Casey, poet, novelist, beautiful human, advocate for a more equal society, cousin and dear friend, who educated and encouraged me in many ways, including the writing of this book.

PROCEEDS FROM THIS BOOK

The entire proceeds of this book (and not just the profits) will go to the Jesuit Refugee Service (JRS), an international organization, working on the ground in over fifty countries, with a mission to accompany, serve and advocate on behalf of refugees and other forcibly displaced persons.

Contents

Lead from the Inside Out

If you wish to lead a good life, reach your potential, lead a team, lead a family, lead a project or an organization, the most important person to first lead is yourself. If you lead yourself well, then you are in a position to lead others, and others will be open to your leadership. You will be leading from the inside out. This book is organized into five numbered sections designed to help you evolve your own personal and collaborative leadership as follows:

1. **Personal Change**: gradually but intentionally manage your own personal and professional evolution, whatever that is for you (and it is different for each one of us).
2. **Personal Leadership**: be happier, healthier, more fulfilled, more effective and efficient, leading yourself by managing your energy, attitude, personality, time and associated tools.
3. **Situational Leadership**: manage well the common situations that occur in teams inside and outside of work, such as meetings, presentations, decision-making, giving everyone a voice and adopting team/group leadership approaches and models that work for you and the situations you encounter.
4. **Collaborative Project Management**: know and practice the typical stages and steps involved in successfully managing a project collaboratively with a team, including the steps for project team members to follow.
5. **Going Further**: use this handbook to deliver a series of workshops for your teams, to gradually improve the leadership, project and management practices of yourself and the groups and organizations you work with.

The intent and intended audience of this book is as follows:

- Individuals who want to lead first themselves and then perhaps others to better places
- Teams who want to collaborate well together
- Organizations that want to be happier and healthier and more collaborative places of work

Origin of this Book

How did this book come into being? In 2010, I published an eBook titled, 'Guide to Collaborative Project Management' and it included one chapter on leadership. Thereafter, it was suggested I write a book, and in 2016 the aforementioned guide expanded into a first edition handbook published on Amazon, still mostly focused on collaborative project management, but with a full and expanded section on leadership. To be honest I had never thought of writing a book and while it was good to get the book out there, as soon as it was published, I could see so much that could be improved!

I then set about writing a second edition of the handbook in 2017 and added full sections on personal and situational leadership. The sections on collaborative project management did enjoy a very positive response but the leadership chapters tapped into a much wider need. You would think I might be content but the same thing happened again. I was happy to have completed the second edition, but I could see more improvements were possible and needed! As explained above, this third edition in 2019 starts with personal leadership and moves out from there – leading from the inside out. This handbook has matured into a mechanism for me to communicate "leadership stuff" I have found useful over the years.

Steve Balmer, formerly CEO of Microsoft, used to say that if Microsoft software was version 3, then it was finally a good product. I hope that the same will be said of this edition of the handbook! You are the judge and I will be interested in the verdict.

With tongue firmly in cheek, I do, however, hope that the advice in this third edition of the book does not go the same way as that of George Harris (1844-1922), US Churchman and Educator, who was addressing students at the start of a new academic year. He said: *"I intended to give you some advice but now I remember how much is left over from last year unused."*

Feedback Please

I hope you enjoy multiple journeys with this handbook. If you journey, please do tell me what you like, would change or believe is missing from this edition of the handbook. I will be happy to listen carefully to all your experiences. Maybe I will need to write a fourth edition of this handbook, so it is even more useful for you and your colleagues! Please send feedback to books@leadinsideout.org.

Éamonn McGuinness,
Galway, Ireland.
24th March, 2019.

Section 1. Personal Change and REP

"Ah, but a man's reach should exceed his grasp, or what's a heaven for?" — Robert Browning

Introduction

This handbook is full of ideas, advice and tips, but how do you make the ones you like real and active for you? How do you make the common sense be common practice, whether you find it in this handbook or elsewhere? The handbook starts by addressing this key question, so you have a pragmatic model to make the desired be real for you, on your personal and professional journey over the coming weeks, months and years. We are all a work in progress, and this handbook helps you figure how to do some of that work! Reaching your full potential, and becoming the best that you can be is a stretch. This book aims to help in this beautiful human quest.

Change Management – Start | Evolve

If you decide that you wish to implement some of the ideas in this handbook, let me add some advice at this point. I am very strong believer in the "Start | Evolve" approach.

Start   **Evolve**

I often see individuals and organizations go from a place of few common practices to a place where they're trying to implement a lot too quickly. An agile approach, where a little delivered quickly with frequent feedback is a stronger and more realistic and reliable method of building sustainable improvement.

3

Some people find it hard to make changes. They get stuck in a rut. As a result, the questions become: How do I get out of it? How do I move? How do I change? This is where "Start | Evolve" really comes into play.

What you really need to do is make a start. Just get some momentum and keep going. Aristotle put it well when he said, "*that which we learn to do, we learn by doing*". In the main, you have to do in order to deeply learn. It's the doing that helps us change. The doing brings us along. This is a very real and pragmatic approach.

Information has a very short half-life. The issue with picking up a new piece of information is unless you do something with it, you forget it very quickly. We tend to confuse reading many books and hearing a lot of stuff with making a change.

One of the other challenges is much of what we hear and read, including what you are reading in this handbook, is common sense, so we tend to say, "*sure, I knew that!*". And, as my father always said to me: "*Common sense, unfortunately Éamonn, it's just not that common!*" Moreover, the reason it is not that common is that we do not practice what we learn. And, if we do not practice what we learn, it does not become a part of how we naturally run. It does not become a part of the way we work. At one level, change is hard, but at another level, when you understand how to change, it becomes easier. Just start. Go for it and do not be afraid to fall.

Please feel confident in selecting and **starting** with a small amount of the advice from this book to implement fast and enjoy early success on your own and/or with your team(s). Then, every week, month or quarter, come back and **evolve** these practices based on feedback and some more of the guidance contained in this book. If you remember this "Start | Evolve" approach, you will get there sooner and better.

How to Use this Book – A Handbook

There is too much advice in this book to implement in one go. This is a real positive! I suggest you read the book once through and then come back later as needed to use this book as a handbook. Perhaps mark with an * the ideas that you feel might be helpful. Feel free to skip chapters you have less interest in on your first read. If there are practices suggested that, you do not like or believe in, then please ignore them! Each chapter represents an actionable chunk of personal or collaborative leadership advice and ends with an implementation exercise. Read and exercise the pieces of this book you believe would be helpful, at a time you believe is relevant. Timing is everything, as they say.

If you do decide to use this book as a handbook and come back for advice and exercises, it is a good idea to keep a journal with your notes and progress. More to follow on this in the paragraphs below.

My real hope is that you will find practical leadership advice in this book to take to benefit from more broadly in your life. I wish you much success in **working** this book in the days, weeks, months and years ahead. To this end, this book is called a handbook!

Change Management and REP

I often see people fall into the trap of making some change with initial success and then stop, so I crafted the "REP" approach.

REP is a play on the word 'repetition'. REP stands for **R**esearch, **E**xecute, and **P**ost-Mortem. REP is a very simple but effective personal change management process.

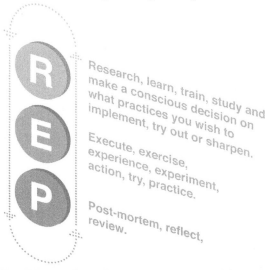

Research, learn, train, study and make a conscious decision on what practices you wish to implement, try out or sharpen.

Execute, exercise, experience, experiment, action, try, practice.

Post-mortem, reflect, review.

We all know that when we repeat something often enough, we tend to get good at it. Now we need to repeat it intelligently. We cannot repeat it the exact same way every time and expect better results. We have to make adjustments. It's like riding a bike. If you ride a bike for weeks and months, you get good at riding a bike. Repetition is an important aspect of mastery.

REP: Research Phase

The "R" phase is where you aim to Research to gain new knowledge. You are seeking best practices. You are looking for great approaches. You are also trying to decide which ones you are going to trial. In this research phase, have fun. Enjoy learning. Love learning. Enjoy researching, looking for new approaches, and looking for new practices. Research can be done in many ways. It can be done online. You can talk to colleagues. You can take some personal and collaborative leadership guidance from this handbook. You have an infinite source of ideas these days and you should enjoy researching them, studying them, learning from them.

As you research, it will be most helpful to keep a REP Journal. You update the REP Journal continuously with notes on anything you liked and thought you would like to try out to see if it might work for you.

At the end of the "R" phase, look through the ideas in your REP Journal and pick a handful. Be realistic! If you have twenty ideas, pick two, pick three or just pick one if that is what you are comfortable with. You must then decide where you are going to trial these ideas. Where are you going to execute? When are you going to exercise?

The output of the "R" phase is threefold: new ideas, new energy, and a decision. The latter is key: a decision on which of the ideas you are going to try and practice. This energy and decision gets you moving, and once you start moving, momentum is now possible.

REP: Execute Phase

The "E" phase is where you Execute these new ideas. You exercise them, try them out, practice them, and experiment with them. The essence of the Execute phase is that you "do it". You try out and prototype the new ideas or practices to see what works. Ideally, you lean back on the wisdom in the Research phase and call on your manager, coach, or mentor to help you. There is no question if you execute honestly and earnestly, you will be performing better this time than you were the last time. And, you will have succeeded.

One thing to consider in the Execute phase is you do not have to work alone. Think about the people in the world who are at the top of their game. They all have coaches, mentors, friends, a shoulder to cry on, someone to push them, someone to nudge them, someone to question them. They have someone behind them who gives them support. If the best in the world achieve their best with a coach, why wouldn't you have one also? Why not ask someone you believe in and trust to be your coach. You deserve a coach – we all do.

RE**P**: Post-Mortem Phase

The "P" or Post-Mortem phase is where you ask yourself, "*How did these new ideas work for me, compared to my intention?*" You should celebrate and enjoy any success in the Execute phase. However, you should not rest on your laurels. You need time out to reflect. You need to think through which ideas and practices worked really well and which could have worked better (if any). It will be very helpful to write these reflections in your REP Journal.

One of the challenges with making a change is people do not take the time to research new approaches. Those that do are ahead. Another challenge we have is that of the many people who do the research, not all execute the new ideas. They do not practice. Those who do practice are way ahead. Maybe they are even getting fifty, sixty, seventy percent of the value. The people who find and research new ideas, and execute them, and actually stop to think afterwards become the masters. Keep this in mind and understand that reflection is a very important part of mastery.

At the end of the Post-Mortem phase, you may take a break to celebrate and enjoy your success but you also get ready to start the next REP cycle. It may not be today that you start the REP cycle. It may not be tomorrow or even next month and that is ok. It is repetition after all, so you need to repeat the cycle to improve.

REP Repeatedly

In the Post-Mortem, you reflected on what happened in the Execute phase. You have really learned from this experience. You know what worked and what needs to be tweaked. Now, go back to your Research phase and look at all the ideas you had. Maybe you decided to execute a few and they worked well. There were perhaps four more ideas that you did not execute during your first REP; pick one or two new ideas and repeat the cycle again.

This REP approach can be used to help you adopt and adapt the personal and collaborative leadership practices described in this handbook. REP is designed to improve capability and to foster creativity.

REP your way to success. We all know someone who goes to the gym to do REP's. They get stronger one day at a time and by some miracle, twelve months down the road, they are really fit! When it comes to REP, it is the same principle. It is repetition, repetitio, it is REP. My personal change management suggestion is to REP your way to success. REP your way to achieve your ambitions. REP your way to change. REP your way to happiness. Please remember that this advancement will not happen by accident. Be intentional about how you want to live your life, about how you change, and use REP or some similar pattern to achieve that change.

Always remember, *"You can do anything you want to do in life, you just have to want to do it."*

Long REP Schedule

You can do more than one REP at once and therefore your REPs overlap, but you need to give enough time to complete the three stages of REP. Here is a sample of scheduling REPs in parallel.

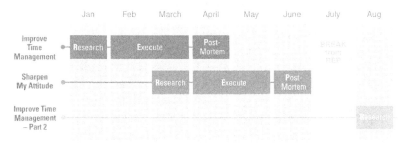

- January: Research phase on your first REP (e.g. Improve Time Management).
- February and March: Execute phase for your first REP (e.g. Improve Time Management). March: Research phase of your

second REP (e.g. Sharpen My Attitude).
- April: Post-Mortem phase for the first REP (e.g. Improve Time Management). Decide if and when you need to do another REP on this topic.
- April and May: Execute phase for your second REP (e.g. Sharpen My Attitude).
- June: Post-Mortem phase for the second REP (e.g. Sharpen My Attitude). Decide if and when you need to do another REP on this area, or if you are good for now.
- July: Take a well-deserved break from REP!
- August: Start the Research phase on your third REP (e.g. Improve Time Management – Part 2).

Shorter REP Cycles

The REP cycles described above are very thorough and quite long. This REP approach might suit your learning style and the situation you find yourself in. You can also try shorter REP cycles, with more frequent iterations. Let us say you want to improve Time Management. You could complete a weekly REP cycle as follows:

- Monday of the first week: Set time aside to do some Research and select a few ideas or practices to try out, and make a note of these in your REP Journal.

- Rest of the week: Execute the selected practices and exercise them for real. Go back to your notes from the Research phase throughout the week as needed for extra guidance.

- Monday of the next week: In a set timeslot, do a Post-Mortem on the prior week and decide how the nominated practices worked. Do you need to focus on them for another week or are you ready to experiment with some new practices? Carry out new Research and select a few extra practices to try out, and again make a note of these in your REP Journal.

- Lather, rinse, repeat. Keep going through this weekly cycle for as many weeks as you find helpful.

In summary, once you get moving with this approach, you are Executing and trying out the practices during the week with a Post-Mortem and a Research phase every Monday. If you REP this way (and I do!), you will start one new practice every few weeks and twenty or more in a year. This is a lot of positive rewarding change.

REP Journal

As mentioned above, it is important to maintain a REP Journal of some sort that suits your style. Perhaps you use a beautiful hard backed paper notebook. These days I use Microsoft OneNote for my REP journal. You can see here that I have pages set aside for each of the key areas that I am currently or have recently REP'ed.

For some areas I am REP'ing, I maintain a simple list on a separate page for each REP area. This page (as depicted below) contains a summary of the key ideas and practices that I liked as part of one of my Research phases for that area. For other areas, I add a serious amount of notes and references to my REP Journal.

As you can see above, I use a tick-box to denote if I am in good shape or not on this desired practice. I also use a star to denote the area that I am currently working and want to better master. As you might guess, there are times when I will un-tick a box where I feel I have regressed or I now believe I have more untapped potential. You might say that one part of my REP Journal is a list of lists. This would be correct!

As mentioned above, for some areas, I fill my REP Journal with copious notes and summaries and links to the area I am researching. I use it as a catalogue of all that I am learning and excited by. It becomes a true research notebook full of wonderful ideas. Then at some point I make a sequenced action list of ideas to execute.

I sometimes also use the REP Journal more like a diary in the Post-Mortem phase and I add comments and thoughts on what worked, what did not work and why. I find great value in this as well. This type of journaling is a super aid to reflection.

REP is an Investment

It is possible that you are saying REP sounds like a lot of work. You are right, it is an investment, but please compare this to other investments you willingly and naturally make. When you go on vacation, have a long weekend with friends or family, buy a new car or bike, get ready for a party, move house, don't you also invest time in planning and working to make these events successful? So why not make an investment in yourself, for yourself to begin with, and an investment that later may help others. Surely, you are worth this REP investment! Of course you are.

With REP, you are gradually building the habits you desire. REP gives you a simple but systematic way to lead yourself to the better version of yourself that you want. Along the way, practices you try out will not work, but this "failure" is not really "failure" but rather movement and feedback that will help your journey.

I practice and enjoy REP (continually using this handbook and a multitude of other sources) for many reasons and especially as REP is a healthy mix of action and reflection. Are you willing to invest in yourself?

"You can't think your way into right action, but you can act your way into right thinking." – Bill Wilson, Alcoholics Anonymous

Connect to Why

If you have a need and a desire to change or improve you will most likely find REP a useful approach. If you have a desire to change but are not managing to do so, then it is helpful and important to connect to your "why". Why do you wish/need to change? Keep asking "why" until you get the answers. This may feel like peeling the many layers of an onion. Get to the root causes. What is your motivation for change? Our motivations are all different. We all live in different contexts. On one level, it does not matter what the motivation for change is, as long as it is real and personal for you. Connect with and remember your "why". This will be powerful.

Time Out

Here are some questions to ponder at this stage:

- Do you feel that you need to make some changes or improvements and what is your why?
- Do you think REP might help you ensure the change and growth you desire?
- If the answer to the previous question is 'yes', are there some areas of your personal and professional life that you wish to or need to REP and when will you start? Why not build REP time into your weekly schedule?
- If the answer to the second question is 'no', can you use some of the REP thinking to devise a personal change management approach that works for you?

Suggestion: Keep notes of this reflective exercise in a REP Journal!

Postscript: The ideas behind REP are simple enough. If you repeat something a number of times, it will get better each time. REP is a neat mix of reflection and action. REP relies on thinking, doing, experience and feedback. So it is with this handbook! I did not wait for the perfect book before going to print. This handbook has been a classic example of REP. Research many ideas and select the ones worthy of inclusion. Express the ideas in a handbook so that I and others can try them. Take feedback and listen to the experience of others and decide what needs improvement/adjusting. Repeat!

Section 2. Personal Leadership

Introduction

This second section of the handbook talks through many facets of personal leadership. The main focus of this section is to assist you leading you for the benefit of you, but there are also extra downstream benefits, mindful of the saying, that you can't (and probably should not) effectively lead others if you can't first lead yourself!

"The most powerful leadership tool you have is your own personal example."
— *John Wooden (1910-2010), UCLA Coach*

Motivation: Why does Personal Leadership Matter?

Why not lead yourself to be the best version of yourself, first for you and then later for the benefit of others you care about or who depend on you? If you are a new team or project manager and you work on these areas of personal leadership, you will be a happier person and you will also be a team or project manager that delivers better results. I would also say the reverse. If you are a manager and you are not in control of the main areas cited in this leadership section, then trouble awaits you around some corner.

The Essence

Meaningful and effective leadership should and does begin with you, for you. However, do not take my word. Please read and judge for yourself. Moreover, if you believe that the information in the following pages is likely to help you personally and professionally, then do take the same REP and "Start|Evolve" approach to the practices in this Personal Leadership section, as described earlier.

Time Out

What aspects of your life/personal leadership are in great shape and worth keeping in great shape? What aspects would you like to work / improve?

Manage Your Energy (Ten Factors)

Introduction

There is a natural relationship between your personal energy levels and your fulfilment from life. This is a very important relationship; the better and the healthier your energy levels are, the more you will get out of your limited time on this earth. Consider this wonderful quote from Aristotle:

"The energy of the mind is the essence of life."

Motivation: Why Manage Your Energy?

Why are we talking about managing your energy in a personal and collaborative leadership handbook? Let me give you one reason. What if you have lots of free time but low energy? Then it is very likely that you are not going to get much done for yourself or others.

This chapter asks five questions on the physical factors and five different questions on the emotional factors that typically affect our energy levels. The chapter also discusses these factors and is bold enough to make suggestions for you. Time-management tips and tricks are covered in the later chapters of this Section 2.

The Essence

If your physical or emotional energy is good (and you can make it so) then anything is possible. However, if your personal energy is low (physically or emotionally) and even if you have all the time in the world, you may achieve very little of what you need or desire.

Time Out

"How good are your energy levels? What gives you positive energy? What drains your energy?"

Take a couple of minutes to do a personal audit and commit to paper how you feel you are doing with your energy levels as you start into this chapter.

Energy Audit: Five Physical Factors

The first part of the energy audit addresses five areas that affect the physical side of your personal energy levels.

Sleep   Diet   Exercise   Breaks   Hobbies

Physical Factor No. 1: Sleep

The first question to ask yourself is: Are you getting enough sleep? Now, obviously, if you are not, there is no way you can have the energy to do all that you need and want to do.

Top performing athletes report that they typically need over eight and a half hours sleep each night. For you, this number could be different and that's fine. It could be six hours or it might be more. Either way, you definitely want to avoid a bad sleep cycle that could go something like this:

- It is late at night and you have not yet done everything you need to do today.
- You are a bit tired and you take some food on-board to get the required energy.
- The food is probably sugar-laden and might include coffee or even alcohol.
- With this new false energy, you stay up a bit later and you get stuff done.
- However, with the extra food in your system, you do not sleep as well as you normally do.
- You then find it harder to get out of bed in the morning; you skip breakfast and you do not exercise. And so the cycle continues.

You need to break a cycle like this. There are many recent studies showing the impact of sleep deprivation and poor sleep quality on our health, energy levels, and work productivity. Every aspect of your life can be improved with more, better quality sleep.

The ideal goal is that you go to bed when you are tired and not much later. Pretty radical, huh? Continuing with the ideal, you do not set an alarm and instead wake up when you are refreshed. Now that may be a stretch and it may take you a while to get there, but this is an ideal scenario to aim for.

The key first question is 'are you getting enough sleep?' If not, what are you going to do about this in order to maximize your energy?

Physical Factor No. 2: Diet

Second question: How is your diet? How are your meals? Do they maximize your energy?

For example, do you start your day properly with a healthy breakfast? Do you eat a reasonable amount of fruit and vegetables throughout the day? Have you a good intake of water? Do you limit your intake of coffee? Do you curb eating late at night, especially large meals? Are you avoiding excessive sugar intake?

We do wonder from time to time what foods are good for us and what not. It is a topic that is covered so widely that my guess is you know already what a good diet entails. It is however no harm to read on the topic, as this research will form a positive part of your change of any eating habits you feel necessary or helpful. You will find no shortage of material on this topic, and I encourage you to open your browser and search and enjoy the research, and then start to eat healthier. Don't wait, start today.

If you do want to dig a bit deeper into this topic, a book that sticks out for me is 'Eat, Sleep, Move' by Tom Rath, who has a rare genetic disorder that has led to cancer in his eye, kidney, pancreas, adrenal glands, and spine. Tom Rath reviewed hundreds of studies to figure out how to slow the growth of new tumors and spread of existing cancers. What he learned about healthy eating (and living) is in this fabulous book.

In summary, does your food intake maximize your energy levels? If not, how are you going to reorganize your time so that you have time to eat and drink properly to give you lots of energy so you can make the most of your life?

Physical Factor No. 3: Exercise

The third question in this part of the energy audit: Are you getting enough physical exercise?

Now, of course you are going to ask, 'What is enough?'. Let me give you a simple definition of enough: more than you did yesterday, more than last week, more than last month. Gradually build it up bit by bit in a safe and healthy way. If you are doing a bit more than before, you are doing enough.

What is the ultimate goal? The goal for the average person is to exercise three to five times per week with each session lasting about thirty to sixty minutes. You should try to get to a level of moderate-to-strenuous exertion in these sessions.

There are many types of exercise; you just need to find the pattern that works for you. If you are fortunate enough to live reasonably close to the office, you can cycle to work as part of your exercise routine. This is a very efficient and healthy use of time. The benefits of exercise are well researched and one such study published in the April 2017 issue of the British Medical Journal[1] reports that *"Cycle commuting was associated with a lower risk of cardiovascular disease (CVD), cancer, and all cause mortality"*. Perhaps you are lucky enough to live by a lake or the sea, as I do, and a swim in the ocean before breakfast is a fabulous way to start your day. Really wakes you up when you are tired, especially in the depths of winter! Perhaps your office is near a sportsground, a wooden area or some walking paths. Maybe you can take a lunchtime stroll. Perhaps you can do some physical exercise at home as you start your day. My daughter pointed me to a phone app, '7 Minute Workout', which I now recommend to you. This is a good all-round set of twelve exercises, especially when you do two or three sets in a row. In any event, find safe and enjoyable exercise that works for you and build this exercise pattern into your daily schedule, if it is not there already. Make this a part of your daily habit.

When you expend energy on exercise, you are going to get a huge amount of energy back, especially if you implement healthy eating and sleeping habits. You will have heard people say that the more you give away without asking for anything in return, the more you seem to receive. It is in giving that we receive. So it is with

---

[1] http://www.bmj.com/content/357/bmj.j1456

exercise. Exercise is one of the gifts that keeps on giving.

Consider this, the day you do not feel like exercising, may well be the day you need to exercise most. Every paper, article, and interview I read on low-moods, stress, anxiety, and depression recommends exercise as part of the get better plan.

In summary, have you time allocated in your schedule for exercise, so you get more energy, and thus get more out of your life?

Physical Factor No. 4: Breaks

The fourth question in the physical factors stakes: Do you take enough breaks? You are probably now saying, 'Éamonn, what is going on? We will soon be talking about making the most of time and you want me to take breaks?!'

Well, ironically, you do need to take breaks during the workday – in the morning, at lunchtime, and in the afternoon – to keep your energy levels up. Sitting for too long is known to cause many health problems and can also really drain your energy. Get up from your desk and walk about during the day. Have standing or walking meetings. Spend a minute or two stretching at your desk. Some people enjoy and benefit from a short nap during the day. Go outside and get some fresh air.

You also need to take breaks away from work in the evening and at the weekends. Ideally, every four to six weeks, you get away for a day or two and do something completely different, a real break. And you certainly need an annual vacation. Maybe you can take a longer sabbatical break from work every few years.

Taking breaks throughout the day, the week, the month, and the year will help you discharge and recharge, and give you more energy. Breaks work!

Ask yourself – 'do you take enough breaks?' Does your typical schedule facilitate real breaks, so that you can maximize your energy and get the most out of your time?

Physical Factor No. 5: Hobbies

Fifth and final question in the physical factor energy stakes: Do you have hobbies? I do not mean work related hobbies, rather hobbies that take you to a different physical and mental place. Maybe it is music, comedy, tennis, golf, football, film, theatre, gardening, community work or the beach. Can you go to a different physical and/or mental place that really takes you away from your work?

We live in very busy times, where it might seem as if we have no time for hobbies. However, the positive energy you will get from a hobby will help you be a happier person and will as a consequence will help make the rest of your life go better. It will be a worthwhile investment.

You might be wondering what hobbies are right for you. I guess the only way to find out is to try a few. Make a list of candidate hobbies and find some time to try one of them at a time until a hobby clicks with and for you. With a bit of research and trial you will find a hobby that floats your boat and that fits into your schedule somewhere. Give it a shot!

In summary, do you have hobbies that give you energy and life? If not, how are you going to adjust your time usage, so that you find and then build in space for such hobbies?

Physical Factors: Summary

How did you do in this audit? If you scored a perfect five out of five, then you are in great shape and you can consider yourself exceptionally lucky. You are in a significant minority.

If, however, you are like most of us and have room for improvement (the biggest room in the house, as they say) then take time out to decide how you will address one or more of the physical factors you believe are important for your better energy management.

I am in no way trying to say that these five physical factors are the only ones that affect your energy levels – so please do extrapolate and use these questions to prompt further personal reflection on any other physical factors that may be draining your energy.

Energy Audit: Five Emotional Factors

The second part of the energy audit addresses five areas that affect the emotional side of your energy, which in turn can have a real effect on your personal energy levels.

Career & Work Choices   Negative Emotions   Gratitude & Reflection   Relationships   It's Not All About You

Emotional Factor No. 1: Career and Work Choices

First question: Are you happy with the career and work choices that you have made thus far?

Some people say to me, 'Éamonn, work is not that important.' I am afraid that I cannot agree. You work from pretty much nine am to five or six pm each day, and many of us probably longer. You do this from Monday to Friday and some of us work at weekends. You do this for roughly forty-eight weeks of the year. Some people sadly more. You do this from age eighteen, nineteen, or twenty-two to age sixty or sixty-five or seventy. You are giving the best hours, the best days, the best weeks, and the best years of your life to work. You have no better time to give.

It is madness not to be happy at work. It is crazy not to enjoy work. If this is the situation you are in, and many people are, then you should do something about it. Change the work you are doing in your current job or change jobs or change career. This may take time – but invest this time.

My brother did just this, quit his job and went back to college at age nearly fifty. Don't tell him I told you! He accepted responsibility. He changed so that he will do something very different for the next fifteen years or so. He is definitely happier. What a way to go. A fabulous example to us all.

If, on the other hand, you are happy in your career and you are happy with your work choices, what are you doing to invest in your career? What are you doing to make the most of it? If this is the best time of your life, what are you doing to absolutely maximize your happiness and your success at work? What is your career investment plan, and how are you fitting this into your schedule and time management approach? What do you want from life? This time will pass. How do you want to look back on this period of your work? A searching but very important set of questions!

Dan Pink, a great thinker and a wonderful author, has written lots about what motivates us at work. He cites three factors: autonomy (the desire to be self-directed), purpose (doing work that makes a difference beyond ourselves) and mastery (the wish to get better at something important to us). Malcolm Gladwell in his truly engaging book, "Outliers", cites three factors that produce meaningful work: autonomy (being in control of our own choices), complexity (mastering skills) and a direct connection between effort and reward (might be financial, spiritual or other). Combining the research of these great thinkers gives us four factors for meaningful and motivating work: autonomy, mastery/complexity, purpose and a direct connection between effort and reward.

Where does your work stand on these four elements? When you go to work, are you fulfilling a contract to get paid or are you building a rewarding career or are you fulfilling a true calling? Which is it – contract, career or calling – and which do you want it to be? And what are you going to do about this? The answers to these tough questions will have a signifiant bearing of your emotional energy.

Emotional Factor No. 2: Negative Emotions

Second question: Do you have a coping mechanism to deal with strong negative emotions? For many people, strong negative emotions are more regular than they desire given their personal situation, their work situation, and sometimes their personality.

In some cases, these strong emotions are often necessary to help us move to where we need to be. Sometimes these emotions are signals that are trying to rock us to a different place. When we hit a hot surface or put our finger on a cooker, we take our finger up quickly. We know what to do. The sudden heat from the hot surface is a signal to act. What is your equivalent with strong negative emotions? Do you know what to do? What is your approach to dealing with strong negative emotions? If we let these emotions fester, they will sap all our energy and we will not be able to deal with the real situation at hand.

There is a most beautiful poem called "The Guest House" by Rumi that starts with these lines … "*This being human is a guest house. Every morning a new arrival.*" The poem goes on to talk about the arrivals, "*A joy, a depression, a meanness*". In the middle of the poem, Rumi suggests we "*treat each guest honorably. He may be clearing you out for some new delight.*" The poem advises we "*meet them at the door laughing, and invite them in.*" The poem concludes by saying, we should "*Be grateful for whoever comes, because each has been sent as a guide from beyond.*" A poem worth reading, enjoying and reflecting on.

We need to acknowledge the strong negative emotion and recognize, 'this is a signal, it is a message, I need to and can do something about this'. We can then apply our energy to doing something constructive about the situation, rather than staying too long in a state of stress and anxiety. If we can do this and I know it is hard, and sometimes it is very difficult, then we are on a restorative path.

One way to work with strong negative emotions is to use a "**Receive, Review and Reframe**" approach.

- **Receive** the negative emotion. At one level, you have very little choice here. A negative emotion sometimes arrives, whether you like it or not. In this "Receive" stage, you acknowledge that this is indeed a negative or difficult emotion. You become more aware and mindful of the negativity. As of yet you have not done much with the negativity, but being aware and acknowledging the negativity is an important first step.

- **Review** the negative emotion to see what it is telling you and to figure where it is coming from. You may not like what you discover but at least you will know. You can and should reflect on why this situation is giving you such grief. Go to the root cause. Why are your feelings negative at this point? There is usually a reason – justifiable or not. Figure why this strong emotion has come to visit.

- **Reframe**, realign, or refocus. You can of course stay in the negativity, but this is not healthy for you and generally, it is not productive. So now that you know what is causing the negativity, what is your course of action, what are you going to do. Armed with this new knowledge you have a choice, you do not have to be stuck in the negativity. Bring yourself to a healthier state.

Some emotions can be so overpowering for us that any rational thought process is unlikely. One way to deal with the immediate effect of such strong negative emotions is to seek a positive distraction. This can be music for some people. Others keep a list of online motivational talks to visit for inspiration from time to time. I myself love music, a great mood changer, and I also find a period of sustained calm breathing outside in the fresh air helpful.

In one of John Powell's more famous books, 'Why am I afraid to tell you who I am?', there is a wonderful quote that neatly summarizes what I am trying to say here; *"your emotions and how you deal with them will probably make or break you in the adventure of life."*

I am not suggesting for a minute that the few paragraphs above are the complete answer, but let me give you the questions and you can then go find the answers that are right for you. The questions are … 'Do you get strong negative emotions? Do they hold you back? Do they take too much of your energy? If so, do have you a coping mechanism? If not, can you develop ways to deal with this?' Not a trivial set of questions I know, but these are very important questions in terms of your energy levels. We will revisit this topic in the next chapter, 'Sharpen Your Attitude to Life (Nine Elements)'.

Emotional Factor No. 3: Gratitude and Reflection

Third question in the emotional stakes: 'Do you take time out to practice gratitude and reflection?' This can be very simple. Some people will achieve this with meditation and other people have similar practices. Are you doing something like this?

Let me explain some more. Do you ever find from time-to-time that you, as they say, smell the coffee and you love the smell? You stop and smell the roses? Maybe a friend came through for you.

Perhaps you really notice the wonderful colors of nature. Maybe you experience a glorious sunrise or sunset. You just happen to look and you say, 'Oh my God, isn't life great?'. Whenever this happens, you get great energy and you feel good. You get a rush. You get peace.

If this is the case, why wouldn't you take time out periodically to recreate this feeling? Maybe invest five to ten minutes of every day to practice reflection and gratitude and get this positive energy. What would this kind of practice look like? Here are three simple steps:

– Firstly, and critically, you start this process by expressing gratitude for at least one good thing in your day so far, and savor the good feeling of this positive memory.

– Secondly, you then reflect on how the day has proceeded so far, the good and the bad, by rummaging through the day, hour-by-hour, or activity by activity since you got up. As you remember each item, you might move on quickly or you might reflect on some more carefully. Maybe you are happy with how you managed each situation and maybe not. Perhaps with the benefit of hindsight, you could have handled some of the situations better.

– Thirdly, decide how you want the rest of the day to proceed, mindful of what you are grateful for and what you learned from looking back on today so far.

A daily process like this can give you bundles of energy. If you think about it, if you are convinced that you should do some physical exercise and you see the benefits, why wouldn't you invest in some emotional or mind exercises? Why wouldn't you give five or ten minutes every day or every few days to such an Examen[2], to such a reflection? With this kind of practice, you get the benefits of more energy to make the most of the precious time you have.

Emotional Factor No. 4: Relationships

Fourth set of questions: 'Do you spend enough time with family and friends in nurturing relationships? Do you have a shoulder you can cry on? Are you a shoulder your friends can cry on? Do you have someone you can talk to? Do you have someone to share your frustrations and joys with?' Very important questions from both an emotional and energy point of view.

As humans, there are things we do really need to talk out. Often, we are thinking things in our head and when we say them aloud to another person we then figure, 'Oh that is not what I meant at all.' This can sometimes happen as soon as the words come out of our mouth! The very act of verbalizing our thoughts is often instructive. Just having somebody to bounce stuff off can be very helpful.

As you are thinking this through, consider the opposite question: "Are there people in your life that sap your energy, who make you feel down?". You need to be careful to avoid these people if at all possible or, if this not possible, have a coping mechanism. My grandfather used to say, 'Show me your friends, and I will tell you who you are". This speaks to the affect our relationships have on our character and temperament. I assume he might also agree with the following: 'Tell me how are your friends, and I will likely know how you are".

So, a question well worth considering: Do you spend enough time in nurturing relationships with family and friends?

Emotional Factor No. 5: It is Not All about You!

Fifth and final factor in the emotional stakes is headlined: 'It is not all about you.' Consider the following: Are there times in your day, week, month, and year when you give to others without counting

---

[2] This simple 3-step practice is an adaptation of the Examen as introduced by Ignatius of Loyola in his landmark book, 'The Spiritual Exercises', from 1548.

the cost? Where you look after folks that need your help? Are you giving of yourself to others?

Perhaps right now is not a time in your life when you can do this outside of work. Maybe you have young children or a sick relative and every spare second needs to go into them as is appropriate. This is your very generous giving to others. Don't worry if you cannot give much time to others outside of work.

Maybe there are folks at work you can help when they are not expecting it. If you are helpful to others, you will typically get their gratitude in return and most likely feel better as a result.

The fifth question in summary: Is there a piece of you that privately and unselfishly gives to others and without ego? Apart from the fact that this is the right thing to do, this will typically help increase your energy levels.

Emotional Factors: Summary

How did you do with these five factors on the emotional side? If you got the perfect score, you are the unique living saint. If you scored poorly, then welcome to the club. You are a human like the rest of us and you have nothing to worry about. However, you do have items to work! These five emotional factors are not the only ones that affect your energy levels – so please do extrapolate and use these questions to prompt further reflection and then action.

Early Mornings and the Habit of Positive Energy

You may well be wondering where to start with better management of your personal energy. Much of this comes down to habit and discipline. If you get into the habit of positive energy practices, then you will have better energy. Not always easy, I know. One way to make a start is to give the very first part of your day to the practices that you select as helpful for your energy levels. In the Irish language, we have an old saying, "Tús maith, leath na hoibre" ("a good start is half the work").

I have selected five practices that I now know are helpful to jumpstart my day in the right way and I get up at 5:15am to do just this. These are: (i) an exercise/prayer for the spirit, (ii) a physical body workout, (iii) a sea swim, (iv) an affirming visualization exercise for the mind and (v) learning something new for fun and to exercise the brain muscle. I call this my "5 at 5:15". I am doing it long enough that is now part of my habit/routine. This early rise at 5:15am is not a macho thing, it is purely pragmatic. Trust me, I do not get up at this time for the sake of getting up early! In order to properly fit in these five items and then a shower and a good breakfast and to be at work for 8am, I need to start by rising at this time.

Exactly what I do in the early morning and exactly when I do this is not so important and is provided here by way of one example. Indeed, the specifics of my routine tend to change every six or nine months. What is important is that I want better energy and I give the first and best part of my day to helping in this quest. I find this really helpful. This works.

If you believe that the amount of energy you enjoy is important to your physical and emotional wellbeing, why not consider making this the first investment of your day, before the day runs away from you?

Summary of Manage Your Energy

This chapter started with a quote from Aristotle:

"The energy of the mind is the essence of life."

What this chapter is aiming to do is help you unlock extra energy (physical and emotional) to make the most use of your time and life. To help unlock this hidden energy that you have the chapter has discussed and asked questions on:

- five physical factors to help your energy levels
- five emotional factors to improve your energy levels
- an early morning energy investment routine.

Questions for an "Energy" REP

<u>Start</u>: If you have conducted a personal energy audit, you will likely have identified a few areas for improvement. Pick one or two suggestions for when you are ready or feel the need to REP this area.

<u>Evolve</u>: Return to this chapter periodically and REP the other energy factors you deem helpful.

Sharpen Your Attitude to Life (Nine Elements)

Introduction

"Whether you believe you can do a thing or not, you are right."
— Henry Ford

I have loved and used this quote for years, but it may not have originated from Henry Ford at all! The quote certainly epitomizes the attitude of Ford, but I can find no verifiable reference or citation. In researching for this handbook, I did see one similar quote by Virgil in "The Aeneid" that reads *"Possunt, quia posse videntur (They can, because they think they can)."* My Latin teacher would be pleased! Let's assume someone way wiser than you or I crafted this "Henry Ford" saying, and let's enjoy it, wherever it came from.

Motivation: Why Sharpen Your Attitude to Life?

Imagine that your next assignment is very challenging. You are thinking about the team members you have joined up with. One person exudes a very positive attitude and the next person has an average enough attitude, as best you can tell. Whom do you look forward to working with? All other things being equal, this is an easy enough question to answer. Attitude really matters. At work or in our personal life we do not know for sure what is coming next. It is best if we ourselves and the people around us have a healthy attitude so we are able to deal with and navigate the natural ups and downs that life throws our way.

The Essence

At work, with your family and in life more broadly, you have the cards you have for now. Maybe you dealt the cards to yourself or maybe someone else dealt them. What matters now is how you deal with the hand of cards you have. In this regard, your attitude really matters. If you wish to be a leader first for yourself and then for others – whether you are the manager or not – it is important that you exhibit a healthy attitude. You want your attitude to be more of a growth mindset than a fixed mindset. You need to recruit more of your brain to help this shift.

Viktor Frankl in his famous and fabulous book, "Man's Search for Meaning" (that I highly recommend), wrote from his World War Two concentration camp experiences (situations infinitely worse than we will ever face): *"what alone remains is 'the last of human freedoms' – the ability to choose one's attitude in a given set of circumstances."* Attitude is a choice. We have the freedom and power to choose.

A healthy attitude is not something that we easily attain. For most of us mere mortals, attitude is something we have to grow, nurture, and sharpen from time to time, which thankfully is very doable.

Time Out

Ask yourself these four deep questions, the three Hs and the potential question.

-Are you **happy**?
-Are you **healthy**?
-Are you **helpful** to others?
-Are you reaching your full **potential**, or on track to do so?

Making the Attitude Investment

If you answered 'Yes' to the four questions above, you are very fortunate and I suspect you are intentionally investing in yourself. And if this is the case, then you are sadly in the minority. If you answer 'No' to some of these questions, let me ask you a final question for now. Are you prepared to invest to turn some of these 'No' answers to 'Yes'? If you answered 'Yes' to this last question, then this chapter has ideas for you.

Attitude and Habits

There are many practices in the other chapters of this handbook that will help you transform some of the above 'No' to 'Yes' answers. If I had to select one chapter in particular, it would be "Manage Your Energy (Ten Factors)". This last chapter could also have been labeled "Get Happy and Healthy" (or combined with this "Attitude" chapter, it might be called "A Path to Resilience"). The "Manage Your Energy" chapter discusses very helpful and practical investments for you to consider, starting with five physical factors:

- Sleep well
- Eat healthily
- Take physical exercise
- Enjoy breaks
- Give time to non-work hobbies.

The chapter continues with five emotional factors:

- Be happy with your career
- Manage negative emotions
- Practice gratitude and reflection
- Invest in healthy relationships
- Give of yourself to others.

The two upcoming chapters on Time Management suggest many useful practices including:

- Set and reset personal and professional goals
- Make the best use of your time with schedules and routines
- Have a coach / mentor to accompany you.

The next chapter, "Know Your Personality (Two Great Mirrors)", introduces two models, The Enneagram and The Myers-Briggs Type Indicator®, to help you understand your personality profile, strengths, traps and leadership preferences. How you are wired and what you do with that wiring definitely affects your attitude.

Take Your Own Drugs

Intuitively we know that many of the practices above can and do help us become healthier and happier. But there is now research on the brain to explain how this comes about. I was never much good at Biology at school, but I am now fascinated by the recent advances in understanding the physiology of the brain and its relationship to psychology. The brain communicates with itself by sending out chemical information - neurotransmitters - from one neuron to another. The brain is like a chemist, naturally producing drugs. The chemicals we hear most about are dopamine, serotonin, endorphins, oxytocin and cortisol. Here follows a very simple explanation from a non-scientist!

Dopamine: We are learning that low levels of the chemical dopamine are associated with self-doubt, lack of motivation, and low self-esteem. We also know that dopamine is associated with pleasure and reward. Dopamine is released when we achieve a goal we have set for ourselves. This helps us understand the *"success breeds success"* phenomenon; we all enjoy the excitement of a reward. Therefore, it is good practice to set smaller, near term goals to increase the levels of dopamine flowing in the reward network of the brain. It is also fascinating to note that with each surge of your own drugs, the brain creates more receiving stations. This means that the next success will have an even bigger effect. Success breeds success, and now we know why!

Serotonin: Research is also teaching us that high levels of the chemical serotonin are associated with people who have meaning and purpose in their lives. Serotonin is known as the 'happy molecule' and is associated with a positive outlook on life. The research also explains that practices such as gratitude release more serotonin into the brain. This is another reason (as if you need one!) to practice gratitude and reflection as suggested in the previous chapter.

Endorphins: You have likely heard of endorphins and runners high. These chemicals are released in response to pain and stress. Endorphins, a naturally occurring chemical, trigger a physical response similar to morphine. If you smile, laugh, and exercise more, you will release your own endorphins.

Oxytocin: And then there is oxytocin, also known as the 'love hormone'. Oxytocin is released by giving and receiving more hugs each day. On a similar vein, there is a wonderful longitudinal study running out of Harvard in Boston on the subject of adult development and what makes a good life. You will find a great talk on TED (November 2015) by Robert Waldinger explaining this study and the findings. The study shows that healthy relationships are the largest influencing factor for a longer, healthier life span.

Cortisol: Not all naturally occurring chemicals are helpful in the long term. For example, cortisol, the chemical the brain produces when we are under stress, kills neurons. Cortisol is part of our 'fight or flight' reaction to threats and stress, and the associated loss of feeling in control. The production of cortisol should stop when the threat passes. Unfortunately, our busy, fast paced lives often mean that the flow of cortisol is constant as we are frequently stressed, which can lead to anxiety, depression, and other health problems. However, the good news is that research also tells us that we can grow new neurons in the hippocampus part of the brain. Serotonin and oxytocin also both reduce cortisol levels. Amazing really.

In summary, there is a strong correlation between the chemicals being released in your brain and the good habits you adopt, so the fuzzier area of your psychology is greatly helped by your actual physiology.

Why Attitude?

So why do we need a separate chapter on 'Attitude' in this handbook? We now know that attitude and good habits are interlinked. Consider this cycle:

– Take on some of the good habits you find in this handbook or elsewhere and your attitude will improve
– Invest in a more positive attitude and it will be easier to adopt good habits
– Lather, rinse, repeat.

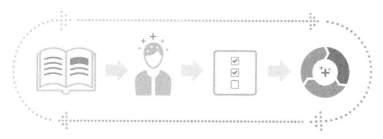

You may read the practices suggested in these chapters and like them but still do nothing with them or at least do nothing substantial. In some of these cases, a healthy attitude will be the key needed to help you unlock and remove the blocks within. And very often many of the blocks are within. My mother sent me a note one day from a sports broadcaster quoting his mother: *"The miles are ahead of you, but the blocks are within."* And as we know, mothers know best!

Nine Elements of Attitude

Let's assume that you would like to adopt some or perhaps many of the suggested practices in this handbook as routine habits. How do you get to a place where you are naturally practicing these habits? Attitude has a massive part to play. The next logical question becomes, how do you sharpen your attitude over time? Here follow nine elements of attitude for you to consider and work.

1. Find Your Motivation

It is typically hard to make a change of any significance without some motivation. The bigger the change desired, the larger the motivation required. Can you think of any reasons that you wish to change your attitude? Find your motivation. Ask yourself, "what is my why?".

A good place to start could be the answers to the four questions in the reflective exercise above. Maybe you want to be happier? Perhaps you wish to be healthier? Or you would like to be more helpful to others (e.g. family, friends, work colleagues, less fortunate, etc.)? Might it be you believe that you are not yet reaching your full potential? As you remember these answers, keep asking yourself 'why' until you get to the root reason, the real why. What is it that you really want and why is this? True motivation will typically help trigger an attitude change. This motivation can be the foundation from which you start to sharpen your attitude.

2. Have a Life Purpose

One of my sisters often says "*that is the honors course!*" when we talk about something challenging. This harps back to a time when we could elect to take some subjects at school at a 'pass' or 'honors' level. The 'Life Purpose' question is definitely the 'honors course'!

If you dig deep enough and search long enough, you might well find a life purpose. This requires a personal investment. Your purpose may adjust or even change as you navigate life. It may change as you and your circumstances change. If you can find and be guided by a life purpose, for a few months or years at a time, then your path through life will be typically be accompanied by a healthier attitude.

I was in Dallas airport on a short stopover from Boston heading to Mexico City for work when I spotted a book called "The Power of Purpose" by Richard J. Leider. I bought the book, read it and 'worked it' on that business trip. It asked me some great questions. Sometimes all you need is the space to answer questions for yourself. To be honest, I had forgotten about the book until writing this paragraph, as this was almost twenty years ago. I found the book and I see my own purpose written in the book, which interestingly enough has remained pretty much the same since. Today I do wonder will it remain so for the next twenty years. I can still see myself sitting in the sun in the back of Luis and Gloria's house in Mexico City answering these questions. I well remember this very positive experience.

If you can answer the 'Life Purpose' question or begin to answer it, then your attitude will get a lift for sure. If you cannot or are not ready to, then have no fear, as this may come to you later. However, do go back to the prior section on "Find Your Motivation", as this will be of help in sharpening a healthy attitude for you.

3. Can Do, Take Responsibility

I have a friend, Neil, who once explained to me that being responsible means being able to respond. Neil does not remember saying this, but it has stuck with me.

There was a saying among some of the older generation in Ireland when I was growing up that suggested *"what is for you, will not pass you by"*. The response from the younger Irish generation was more akin to *"if it is to be, it is up to me"*. I was very fortunate to be close to both of my parents and to two of my grandparents (one from each side of the family) and they were definitely in the latter camp. I can still remember the tone of my grandmother's voice as she quite forcibly explained to me, at the age of five, *"there is no such thing as you can't"*. I found out since that she was right! I will be forever grateful for both this insightful lesson and the vivid memory. Later I modified this lesson into my own version: *"you can do anything you want to do in life, you just have to want to do it"*. This, of course, brings us back to the motivation question from the last few paragraphs.

It is very important to be persistent, to persevere. There is such a thin line between what is perceived as success and what is perceived as failure. Never give up if your dream or goal is important to you. Why should you? Perseverance pays. Push yourself. Be ambitious. Take the long view. Reach for your potential. You can.

I ask you to consider the following. You are responsible for your own desired outcomes. You are able to respond. You do not have to accept the status quo. You need to adopt a 'can do' attitude for a healthier, happier and more fulfilled life. You need to take personal responsibility as a key part of your personal leadership. You need to cut the excuses and just get on with it.

4. Invest in Good Habits

The good news – you can sharpen your attitude. The realistic news – your attitude may not change dramatically overnight. If you successfully adopt some of the practices in this handbook as relevant for you, you will build confidence and sharpen your attitude. To sustain this level of sharpened attitude, you need to keep up the practices. Consider this like any other investment you make. You need to sow in order to reap. You need to make the good habits habitual. Success will breed more success.

It is also important to remember that your habits, good and bad, and how you interact with the world can have a positive and sometimes a negative effect on those around you at home and at work.

There are various studies on how many days or months it takes to adopt a new practice and make it a habit. In reality there is no one answer as it depends on many factors, e.g. how hard the practice is for you, how motivated are you, etc. Think how long you needed to learn how to walk or ride a bike or drive a car. Mastery requires repetition. For the purpose of this section, let's propose the following investment rule of thumb:

– Easy habit: twenty days
– Difficult habit: thirty days
– Very difficult habit: sixty days
– Extremely difficult habit: ninety days (or longer).

I believe it is important to acknowledge that you need to invest enough time to make a worthwhile habit stick. Of course, you will fall off the wagon from time to time, but generally speaking, it will not take as much time the second or third time around to adopt the same habit. So don't give up! Maybe consider this three-step process to forming a new habit:

i. Set a specific **goal**
ii. Set aside a designated and suitable **time** each day to bake this practice into your routine
iii. Set **rewards** along the way, to enjoy the fruits of your efforts.

A healthy attitude helps you take on difficult and new challenges. A healthy attitude helps you deal with life. A healthy attitude is built on the foundation of good habits. As was explained above, this is an iterative investment process:

- Adopt the attitude that you will take on helpful practices as habits
- Take on these new habits and your attitude will sharpen again
- Lather, rinse, repeat.

A sharpened attitude does not come for free. You will need to invest, and adopting good habits is a great investment to help sharpen your attitude.

5. Think Positive Thoughts

We are our thoughts much of the time. We owe it to ourselves, and those near and dear to us, to make these thoughts and therefore ourselves as positive as possible.

We are learning from research that the brain naturally generates more negative thoughts than positive thoughts – maybe by a factor of four to one, depending on the person and the place they are at in life. Because of these learnings, psychologists are explaining that we need to generate more positive thoughts to counteract naturally occurring negative thoughts. The issue is further complicated by the fact that some of these negative thoughts have a large impact, often more significant than one single positive thought. Therefore, we need three, four or even five times as many positive thoughts as negative thoughts to put ourselves in a good place.

So what is happening in the brain? Physiology explains that the neurons fire and then wire together – not always in a good way. Our normal wiring or natural way of reacting is not always positive. The good news is that we can in time rewire the neurons in our brain to react in a healthier manner. I just love this, we can rewire the brain. We do not have to be stuck with attitudes that we are unhappy with and some of which may ultimately be harmful.

Think of it this way. We have an emotion that triggers a set of thoughts, which lead to certain behaviors or responses. For example, I am cycling to work and some reckless driver comes quickly out of a side road and cuts across me (the situation). I immediately get a fright and then really annoyed (the emotional response). I start to imagine what I will say to the driver when I catch him at the next set of traffic lights (the thoughts) and I am further enraged (more emotions). When I do eventually catch up, I shout at him (the physical response). In the process, I lose lots of the natural calm and energy that I desired and was enjoying from cycling to work. This is not entirely an imagined situation! It might be hard to avoid these situations (bad drivers) and initial emotions (fright and anger), but I can rewire my response with reflection and experience. This is a choice I have once I realize it.

A little bit more on personal choice. Back in the early 1990s, my mother and aunt invited me to a lecture in the local university by a Dr. William Glasser, who coined the phrase and practice of "Reality Therapy" and wrote a book called "Choice Theory". The example he gave to explain Choice Theory was a patient who was going through a very difficult and stressful marriage breakup. The patient explained that he was depressed. The doctor asked him why. The patient explained that he was depressed because his wife did not love him anymore. The story ended with the doctor agreeing that based on the evidence presented, it was a fact that his wife was leaving and did not love him anymore, but that the patient was choosing to depress. The doctor explained that while the patient could not likely change the fact that his wife was leaving, he could choose how he reacted. It was a fascinating insight. The doctor did not imply that the patient could flick a switch and cease feeling depressed. What he did explain was that somewhere deep down, the depression in this particular case and (and of course not in all cases) was a choice, conscious or otherwise.

This same idea on the power to choose is very cleverly explained in the quote below from an article contained in a 1963 collection called "Behavioral Science and Guidance: Proposals and Perspectives". This explains that after the stimulus and before we make our response, that there is a space to reflect and in this space we have the power to choose what course of action we will take.

This is our choice, our freedom, and also our chance to change, grow and nurture our attitude.

"Freedom is the individual's capacity to know that he is the determined one, to pause between stimulus and response and thus to throw his weight, however slight it may be, on the side of one particular response among several possible ones."
– Rollo May (psychologist), *"Freedom and Responsibility Re-Examined"*.

Let me introduce another source of negative thoughts we encounter. We humans have a tendency to over-judge other humans. And we hang on to the negative thoughts associated with these judgements for too long. It is helpful to remember that an action a person carries out does not define that person. Remember it is more honest to judge and dislike the action but not to judge and dislike the person. It is also wise to remember that we humans are a constant work in progress, and the person you meet today will likely be different tomorrow or next week or next month or next year, so do not be too hasty in passing judgement. This will help you think more positive thoughts and therefore act more positively.

In many ways, we are our thoughts, but we do not have to be, especially if these thoughts are negative or in any way limiting us. I like the line from Deepak Chopra, *"I am a field of infinite possibilities"*. Recent advances in physiology and psychology reveal that we have more control than we knew, as we understand more of what we think and feel. It is much easier to have a healthier attitude when we know how. Understanding this will really help you manage your emotional energy and your outcomes.

We now know that the good habits and practices advocated in this handbook (and in so many other books) release chemicals to make us feel and move better. We also understand we need to proactively counteract the onslaught of negative messages with more positive thoughts. Finally, we recognize that we have more control over reactions to our feelings than we previously realized, and we can actually rewire the neurons in our brains in a positive direction. We can improve our attitude by changing our thoughts in these ways.

If All Else Fails, Get Over Yourself

If the above does not work, let me leave this section with one funny but hopefully insightful story. Not so long ago, I was at a birthday party of a school friend, a fiftieth celebration no less. I only give the age to explain how long it is since we were at school together to give the story its proper context. One of the guys (an extremely successful man in his chosen field) was moaning about some of the teachers at school. In retrospect, I believe he was more having fun than moaning, but his wife overheard. As my friend was pouring forth, his wife interrupted and scolded him as follows: "*you need to get over yourself*". The room erupted in laughter to hear our eminent professional carpeted by his wife in this manner. It was sweet! However, the phrase has stuck with me ever since, as we do need to just get over ourselves from time to time. How right she was!

6. Work the Worries

The prior section explains that we naturally have many, many negative thoughts each day. I emphasize naturally, as this is how the brain is wired. Some of these thoughts are worries about what might happen. These can be positive as they help us avoid the unpleasant or unwanted. We need these worries and fears to cope and survive. However, we do not need to hold onto these worries for too long. We do not want to be paralyzed by the worries. You often heard the expression, "*sick with worry*". I am sure there have been times when you have been sick in the stomach with worry. Doctors tell us that some illnesses are psychosomatic, meaning a physical illness is caused by stresses, strains and emotional factors.

The real worries can often be messages that we have something to work. At some stage we need to decide to ignore the worry and let it go or to work the worry. So when you find yourself getting worried, do not beat yourself up for being worried, and do not stay in the worried state. It is a normal part of the human condition. However, do work the worry as soon as you can. You will generally feel much better once you start to work the worry.

I believe that many of our worries are not very serious, once we think them through. Try to get perspective on your worries. As they say, try not to sweat the small stuff.

I originally called this section "Work Your Worries" but then renamed it to "Work the Worries". Working your own worries is, of course, critical for a healthier attitude. However, this handbook is all about leadership, so it is also important to help others on your team or in your circle to work their worries. This is what a good selfless leader will do. It can also help you personally if those close to you are not so worried, as the general mood and attitude lifts.

7. Fall Upwards

A few years back, I read a book called "Falling Upward" by Richard Rohr. I loved it. It clicked with me immediately. In fact, I have the book marked with stickeys and every now and again, I go back to it.

One of the main points of the book is that we need to fall to grow. A very simple example is that if we fall off a bike when we are learning to cycle, we will generally learn how to ride a bike properly, confidently, and not too cautiously. The book explains that each fall is the fuel needed to grow, if we can see it that way and grab it.

At home, I would have grown up with the *"silver lining in every cloud"* philosophy. In my early career, I learned that we should *"learn from our mistakes"*. I am comfortable that both of these are still true and useful. However, I am increasingly more comfortable with the notion that we need to fall every now and again to grow. *"No pain, no gain"* as the coach used to tell us on the football field. In this case, the pain is associated with failing or what is perceived as failure.

The "Falling Upward" book brings forward some other interesting points. For example, we need to let ourselves off the hook when we fall and we need to forgive ourselves. In this way, we will be more tolerant of the falls that others have and then we will be able to help in their growth. We may need to forgive ourselves and others earlier and more often and this "Falling Upward" understanding and attitude helps.

Life will not always go as you plan. There will be many falls for you. How will you look on these falls? Can you look on them as opportunities to learn and evolve, even when those around you do not have the same perspective? If you can do this, if you can fall upwards in a crowd, then this is a wonderful investment in sharpening your attitude and your future.

8. Be Comfortable with Contradictions

Life can be confusing sometimes. Life can seem contradictory. Just

take a look at some of the suggested practices in this handbook:
- Be action oriented yet reflective
- Make the best use of your time but take lots of breaks
- Invest in yourself but be helpful to others
- Have a successful career but spend more time with your friends and family
- Be successful but learn to fall
- Be intentional on a path but be open to new possibilities
- Be very respectful to people but do not let them off the hook if they do not deliver on expectations.

Life is not black or white. It is the many shades of grey, made up by black and white. I hasten to add that life is also very colorful! The solutions to challenges are not always clear-cut but they are understandable if you think them through. Understand and learn to be comfortable with the contradictions. Make your decisions on where to balance out the contradiction for you. With this level of comfort, you will have a sharper attitude that will stand to you.

9. Be Ambitious for Your Life

Live your life to the full. Be ambitious for your life. Remember, as life is short, it is better to be happy, healthy, and helpful to others, so you can lead your life to the full. Make this an element of your attitude to life. I love the attitude to life expressed in this quote:

> "I want to be thoroughly used up when I die, for the harder I work, the more I live. I rejoice in life for its own sake. Life is no brief candle to me. It is a sort of splendid torch which I have got hold of for the moment, and I want to make it burn as brightly as possible before handing it on to future generations."
> – George Bernard Shaw (1856 to 1950), Irish writer.

Live your life on purpose. Live intentionally. Be the best that you can be. You can't control everything and it is unwise to try. But this is no excuse to drift. Decide what you want from life and what you are prepared to give to fulfill these intentions. You do not have to plan your whole life but do at least think through the next few months and years. What you want from life will change as you journey through life, so you need to be open to new possibilities while remaining intentional in the meantime. If you make the commitment to live intentionally, while remaining open to other possibilities, you will have a sharper attitude to life.

In order to be open to other possibilities, you need to be aware. You need to be present. This is a very important aspect of personal leadership, being self-aware. The ideas and chapters in this section of the book (e.g. reflection and gratitude practices) will definitely help you on this path to greater self-awareness.

Learning and Other Elements of Attitude

Are there more than nine elements of a healthy attitude? Of course there are. I had to restrict myself from writing a list with nineteen elements. However, these nine will get you well started. If you work on some of these nine, you will definitely have a sharper attitude to life. In addition, hopefully these will trigger your curiosity to search for more elements to provision you for your journey. It is important to remember that we only know what we know! It is vital to feed your brain with new information, ideas and thoughts. Seek inspiration from outside as well as inside. Keep learning and you will be sharpening your attitude to life.

We like and often find patterns helpful. GROW is one such pattern that comes to mind, when I think of 'sharpening attitude'. To help sharpen or GROW your attitude you can find it very helpful to:

- Set **G**oals: make some decisions about what you want. Give yourself some specific and relevant motivation.
- **R**EP: take the time to REP (Research, Exercise, Post-mortem) whatever area it is that you feel is necessary for you to REP at this stage of your journey.
- **O**rganize yourself: you can fit more in to life as you get better organized. Work Time Management in your favor.
- **W**ork hard: there are no short cuts, I am sorry to say! Hard work is necessary, and it pays handsome dividends.

Human Values

When we moved into our new house, a family friend gave us a poem that I had not seen before, which is now framed on the wall of our home. I have since learned that the poem titled, *"Children Learn What They Live"*, was first published in 1954 by Dorothy Law Nolte. You may well have seen the poem. It starts with the line, *"If children live with criticism, they learn to condemn*". If you have not yet seen this poem, I recommend you search for it.

I have heard people say that the world would be a better place if adults were more like children. It dawned on me that it would be interesting to reflect on this poem as an adult, as a check on our way of living and as a check against the attitudes and practices we have. With this in mind, here is the poem with the "children" replaced by "I", and with "live" replaced with "practice". With sincere appreciation to Dorothy Law Nolte.

If I practice criticism, I learn to condemn.
If I practice hostility, I learn to fight.
If I practice fear, I learn to be apprehensive.
If I practice pity, I learn to feel sorry for myself.
If I practice ridicule, I learn to feel shy.
If I practice jealousy, I learn to feel envy.
If I practice shame, I learn to feel guilty.

If I practice encouragement, I learn confidence.
If I practice tolerance, I learn patience.
If I practice praise, I learn appreciation.
If I practice acceptance, I learn to love.
If I practice approval, I learn to like myself.
If I practice recognition, I learn it is good to have a goal.
If I practice sharing, I learn generosity.
If I practice honesty, I learn truthfulness.
If I practice fairness, I learn justice.
If I practice kindness and consideration, I learn respect.
If I practice security, I learn to have faith in myself and in those about me.
If I practice friendliness, I learn the world is a nice place in which to live.

Summary of Sharpen Your Attitude to Life

Attitude is everything. The ideas and practices above will help you live life with a sharper attitude. Take responsibility to lead your own life to a place that you are happy with life. Be self-led. Remember, "*You can do anything you want to do in life, you just have to want to do it*".

I will leave the last words of this chapter to Abraham Maslow (American psychologist, 1908 to 1970) of the "Maslow's Hierarchy of Needs" fame:

"If you plan on being anything less than you are capable of being, you will probably be unhappy all the days of your life."

Questions for an "Attitude" REP

Where do you now stand on the idea that you can sharpen your attitude, and that it will not sharpen by accident?

<u>Start</u>: Select one or two of the "Nine Elements of Attitude" to REP when you are ready or feel the need to work this area, perhaps starting with "Find your Motivation".

<u>Evolve</u>: Schedule time to REP some of the other elements.

Know Your Personality (Two Great Mirrors)

Introduction

"I want freedom for the full expression of my personality."

— Mahatma Gandhi

This chapter is intended to help you reflect and focus on how your personality influences your style and approach to life and work, and how to work this! This chapter on personality is intended to help you in both your professional and personal life.

The first five words of this book are "Lead from the Inside Out". It is of course hard to lead from the inside if you do not know the inside. Trying to lead yourself and others without being self-aware is like finding your way out of a large strange location in the dark. It is possible, but it is quite difficult and success is not at all guaranteed.

Motivation: Why Focus on Your Personality?

You have a personality and there is no getting away from it! Who you are and how you are naturally wired affects how you live, love, lead and manage. Your personality, therefore, influences your happiness and success rate in and out of work, sometimes for good and sometimes not. At a very minimum, personality influences your communication style. Your family, friends and team can definitely see your personality. Shouldn't you also be able to?!

The Essence

To fully see yourself in the physical form, you need to use a number of mirrors, each placed at different angles: front, back, side, above, below, etc. So it is with personality. You need different models or mirrors to get to know the real you. However, one good mirror will give you a great start – an incisive first view. You will be amazed what you can see! Even though it is definitely not the "full you", it will be helpful. It will illuminate.

There are a number of different personality models or mirrors you can readily get information on and learn about. I have experience of two in some detail, both of which I like, respect, find very helpful and, most importantly, I trust. I will give a pretty good introduction and explanation of the Enneagram and a very brief introduction to the Myers Briggs Personality Indicator, or MBTI as it is also called. I have covered the Enneagram in some detail as it shed light on aspects of my own personality that I was not as in touch with. This kind of light was and continues to be a real gift.

I know that many people are dubious and skeptical of personality models. If you are in this camp, have a read and hopefully you will get some value from this chapter. I am not for a minute suggesting that you let any personality model run your life, but these models can give great insights to help you make more informed decisions.

Time Out

In your experience, how does or should personality affect or shape your style of Personal and Collaborative Leadership?

Enneagram – A Number

Ennea is the Greek for nine and gramma is a sign. The Enneagram charts nine personality types, as depicted here.

Enneagram – More than a Number

I can hear you say already: there are seven billion people in the world and only nine personality types, no way! And if the nine types were very rigid, then you would of course be right. It is important to stress that which we all know: no two people in the world are exactly the same, yet there are recurring patterns. In Enneagram terms, you are a number (more often called a type), but you are also far more than a number. Each Enneagram type has a rich and deep description. You are typically travelling and living on a spectrum of unhealthy to healthy with your type.

Enneagram – Centers, Wings and Arrows

As you dig deeper into the Enneagram, you will discover that you come from a center and have wings and arrows into other Enneagram types. For example, I belong to the 'Heart' or feeling center (two, three and four) and not the 'Head' or thinking center (five, six and seven) and not the 'Gut' or instinctive center (eight, nine, one). I am a three, influenced by a strong two wing and am influenced to a lesser but real extent by a weak four wing. When I am acting healthily, I tend to act out the more attractive aspects of the six, but when I am very tired, I can move to the less redeeming aspects of the nine. I would not expect you to understand in detail what this means just yet, but hopefully this gives you a sense of the richness of the Enneagram.

In summary, as you research and learn more about the Enneagram, you will discover, enjoy and benefit from a deeper model than is evident on first glance with a single number. Stick with it! The Enneagram is rich with many layers and dimensions.

The Enneagram Decomposed

This chapter will introduce and explain each of the nine types in the following pages. I will speak in the first person, so you can try each of the explanations on for size. I will outline each Enneagram personality type in four short sections: profile, strengths, traps, and a leadership perspective.

In the sections below, I talk about healthy and unhealthy behaviors. When a person is acting from a healthy place, the strengths are deployed. When a person is acting from a less healthy place, we are falling into the traps typical of our personality type. I am a great believer in the idea that we have traps more so than weaknesses. You can see how a confident person (which is a great strength of ego) could talk about themselves too much and put people off (an overuse of ego). The very strength becomes a trap. I often see we fall into repeatable traps when we overuse a strength. It is not much fun to read about and admit the traps. It can and, to an extent should, be very humbling. It is, however, very fruitful to really understand these traps that we tend to fall into so we can avoid them or get out of them quicker. The truth about yourself can set you free.

Type 1 – Perfectionist / Reformer

Profile

I do it the right way. I like to improve myself and everyone else to make the world better, to make the world right, even if sometimes others do not want this!

Strengths

I set very high standards. I am typically compliant with rules. I dot all the "i"s and cross all the "t"s. You can trust me to deliver on my promise.

Traps

I am not that flexible. I can become anxious about stuff that is not going right. I tend to be critical and resentful of others who do not meet my standards. I definitely find that work can become life, and relaxation is missed, unless I am very careful.

Leadership Perspective

I am a very diligent leader who strives for the highest quality possible.

Type 2 – Helper / Giver

Profile

I am motivated to help others. I love being needed and liked, even if I do not admit this to others.

Strengths

I am very generous and caring. I am typically optimistic. I am very attuned to the feelings of others. I build great relationships and I enjoy this.

Traps

I am not very good at looking out for my own needs. I can get angry and badly let down when I feel unappreciated and this will be very evident to all as I wear my feelings on my sleeve. I can be too accommodating and I find it hard to say "No." I can be manipulative if I am acting as the unhealthy me.

Leadership Perspective

I am the servant leader. I enjoy being of service to others.

Type 3 – Achiever / Motivator

Profile

I want to be successful and productive. I am not fond of failure. For me, this is the "f" word!

Strengths

I am very goal driven. I am efficient and energetic. I am a particularly hard worker and I am highly productive. I am a pragmatic problem solver and get stuff done.

Traps

I am not tolerant or appreciative of others who are not achieving. When I am unhealthy, I can act from a place of vanity and ego. I am not always not mindful of the feelings of others. I have no "off" switch. I can act more like a "human doer" than a "human being".

Leadership Perspective

I have a relentless drive for success to deliver or exceed the goals.

Type 4 – Romantic / Individualist

Profile

I want to be connected to my feelings and be understood. I definitely do not want to be ordinary.

Strengths

I am creative and artistic. I am very expressive. I can be inspiring and supportive. I strive for excellence.

Traps

I can swing very high and very low, and can be moody and self-absorbed or have high energy. I am not always great at taking feedback. I can definitely be stubborn at times. I get bored easily and want to move on to the next, more interesting project quickly.

Leadership Perspective

I strive to lead, so that we all experience real meaning and our true purpose.

Type 5 – Observer / Investigator

Profile

I want to know and understand so I can be independent and, of course, not look foolish.

Strengths

I have an admirable thirst for knowledge. I am analytical and a good problem solver. I am able to compartmentalize. I am perceptive and systematic.

Traps

I can appear distant, as if I enjoy my own company. I can be negative and when I am acting from an unhealthy place, please don't ask me to repeat myself! I can undervalue relationships. I am not assertive enough.

Leadership Perspective

I and we need to research, think and know everything, and then we will be more effective on our projects.

Type 6 – Questioner / Loyalist

Profile

I enjoy security, so I tend to fear and prepare for the worst. I am very loyal but do not cross me!

Strengths

I am very responsible and reliable. I am funny and fun to be with. I am practical and a great team player. I am very collaborative, loyal and dutiful to my team, to authority and to my company.

Traps

I can be paranoid and this is exhausting for me. I tend to be controlling and rigid. I am often highly judgemental of others. I can also be indecisive, overly analytical and risk averse.

Leadership Perspective

I like to make sure all the team feel involved, where we can overcome all the obstacles that I see.

Type 7 – Adventurer / Enthusiast

Profile

I like to be happy, do fun stuff and to do good. I am not much into suffering through and I want to keep all my options open!

Strengths

I am fast. I am a quick thinker and I am great in a crisis. I have lots of enthusiasm and exude optimism. I am very productive and I naturally multi-task. I am courageous and not afraid to take risks.

Traps

I can be impulsive. I am not that disciplined. I may not finish what I start. I can be very restless and I like to move on. I can be easily distracted and I am not fond of routine. I am not always focused.

Leadership Perspective

Let me help the team find new and exciting stuff so we will take advantage of this and we do not miss these opportunities.

Type 8 – Challenger / Boss

Profile

I like to be strong and I want to appear so, even if I am not. Please fight back or I will not respect you.

Strengths

I am very confident. I have high energy. I am extremely direct. I am very loyal to the cause, especially if it is a just cause.

Traps

I can be controlling. I like it to be my way or the highway. I am often domineering and this can be intimidating for others around me. I tend to be self-centred and sometimes aggressive.

Leadership Perspective

I am a decisive, take-charge leader who likes strong people in the key roles. Just follow me, have no worries, and we will be fine.

Type 9 – Peacemaker / Mediator

Profile

Generally, I like peace and harmony and I like to go with the flow. I definitely avoid conflict.

Strengths

I am open minded, accepting, empathetic, and non-judgemental. I am well able to relax and have a good time. I am extremely patient. I am a great relationship builder.

Traps

I can be indecisive and not assertive enough. When unhealthy, I am apathetic and then nothing happens. I can be forgetful. I am good at procrastination – in fact, very good!

Leadership Perspective

If we all get on really well and are nice to each other, the work will be accomplished so much quicker.

Which Enneagram Type Are You?

What Enneagram type do you think you are? Only you can tell and it is likely that you do not have enough detail in the preceding pages to know. But, hopefully you are intrigued!

You are very likely finding yourself in many of the types. To help you a little bit on this quest, your type goes to the root cause of why you do what you do. I might appear extremely helpful to others and perhaps this is because I am a 'two' (the helper/giver). Or, maybe it is because I am being paid to be helpful and I want to be successful, so I am acting more of a 'three' (the achiever/motivator). I might spend hours cutting the trees in my front yard to a perfect height because I am a 'one' (the perfectionist/reformer). But perhaps I do this because today it appeals to my artistic side (the romantic/individualist) as a 'four'. The books referenced towards the end of this chapter contain self-tests to guide you on this quest for your type.

Words of warning: please do not assume you know what Enneagram type someone else is and please do not judge someone even if you do.

The Best Enneagram Type?

Is there a best Enneagram type? Absolutely not. The real value of the Enneagram is to know yourself, to be more self-aware, and as a result, act out of a healthier and happier place. As my daughter reminds me from time to time, "*Éamonn, we are here for a good time, not a long time.*" Life is very short and self-awareness is one of the tools that will help you make the most of your life.

The Best Enneagram Type for Leadership?

Let us review the leadership perspectives from the nine types and see if we identify the best type for the role of team/project leader.

1. I am a very diligent leader who strives for the highest quality possible.
2. I am the servant leader. I enjoy being in service of others.
3. I have a relentless drive for success to deliver or exceed the goals.
4. I strive to lead, so that we all experience real meaning and our true purpose.
5. I and we need to research, think and know everything and then we will be more effective at work.
6. I like to make sure the team all feel involved, where we can overcome all the obstacles that I see.
7. Let me help the team find new and exciting stuff, so we

will take advantage of this and we do not miss out on these opportunities.

8. I am a decisive, take-charge leader who likes strong people in the key roles. Just follow me, have no worries and we will be fine.

9. If we all get on really well and are nice to each other, the work will be delivered so much quicker.

Can you spot the perfect leader? I am thinking not. I assume you can see positive leadership and management qualities in each of the nine types. In many ways, the ideal leader is able to deploy any of these fine qualities on any collaborative endeavor.

You will find that some types (e.g. one, two, three, and eight) more often end up in leadership or management positions. However, when any of these types are acting from the unhealthy place of their personality type, the team will likely be challenged.

It is rare enough that personality type is checked before appointment to leadership, so you will find all nine types in leadership and in management positions. The key is to know your strengths and traps, and match them to the context of the specific situation, team or project. For example, as a type one you strive for perfection. How much perfection is needed on this project? As a type two, you will want to help everyone. Do you have time to help everyone on this project? As a type six, you can be indecisive. Is this hurting the project? And so on.

Enneagram – A Brief History

Some readers will wonder where this all came from and for you, this is an extremely short history as I understand it (mostly summarised from the book by Richard Rohr referenced in the next section of this chapter).

Some Enneagram researchers have made links to Pythagoras, the Greek mathematician and philosopher, from the 5th Century BC. There are early references to eight forms of temptation in the 4th Century AD in Egypt, developed by the Desert Fathers. Incidentally, the early Christian Church labeled this as heresy.

Another development appears in the early 14th Century in Spain when Ramón Lull, a lay or tertiary Franciscan, was drawn to Sufism. At this point, we got a 9-point diagram of human characteristics of vices and virtues.

Fast forward to the early 1900s when George Ivanovitch Gudjieff, an Armenian spiritualist, did more work on the model, describing features covering our true essence. In the early 1960s, Oscar Ichazo, a Bolivian spiritual teacher, developed personality descriptors. In the 1970s, Claudio Naranjo, a Chilean-born psychiatrist, adopted the Enneagram in California. Jesuits in the US (including Fr. Robert Ochs SJ) worked on the model with Naranjo, adopting the Enneagram for retreat work and spiritual guidance.

As you can see, the model has a rich history over the centuries and has been developed by people of many different faiths and none. The Enneagram crossed the divide in the US from the spiritual to the business world and is now used by many corporations around the world as a leadership development tool focusing on that critical aspect of leadership, self-awareness.

I should add that I am no historian and the above is an indication of the deep and varied roots of the Enneagram rather than an exact history. If you are interested in the history of the Enneagram, maybe you can use this as a starting point to search for the more detailed story.

In 1985, I was going on a vacation to Berkley, CA and my uncle was driving me to the airport. On that two-hour journey, he introduced me to the Enneagram. I walked the streets of Berkley in September 1985 and eventually found a store called "Shamballa" where I bought my first book on the Enneagram. I was hooked!

Here was a model that knew me better than I knew myself. The Enneagram is a mirror that I have returned to over the years and it has always been a great teacher for me.

Enneagram Books

There are many sources of reliable information on the Enneagram. I have bought, read, loaned, and lost many books over the years but here is a list of some the Enneagram books currently on my shelf.

- "The Enneagram Made Easy: Discover the 9 Types of People", by Renee Baron and Elizabeth Wagele
- "Discovering Your Personality Type: The Essential Introduction to the Enneagram", Revised and Expanded by Don Richard Riso and Russ Hudson
- "What Type of Leader Are You? Using the Enneagram

System to Identify and Grow Your Leadership Strengths and Achieve Maximum Success", by Ginger Lapid-Bogda
- "Bringing Out the Best in Everyone You Coach: Use the Enneagram System for Exceptional Results", by Ginger Lapid-Bogda
- "The Enneagram: A Christian Perspective", by Richard Rohr.

I am happy to recommend all of the above, but if you are new to the Enneagram, I would start with the first one on the list. It is a fun, easy introduction, and the one I give to my family, co-workers and friends as a starter.

The Myers Briggs Personality Types

I have explained above that the Enneagram is a very helpful mirror, one of many such mirrors. The Myers-Briggs Type Indicator (MBTI) is another such instrument that I find extremely insightful and helpful. The MBTI was developed by mother and daughter, Katharine Briggs and Isabel Myers, in the 1940s and 50s, extending Carl Jung's theory of psychological type from the 1920s.

Carl Jung gave us **E**xtrovert or **I**ntrovert, **S**ensing or i**N**tuition and **T**hinking or **F**eeling (see below for a brief explanation of these). The Myers Briggs extends Jung's work by developing the MBTI instrument to help us see patterns in how we prefer to use our perception and judgement. Perception is how we come to knowledge, whereas judgement is how we come to conclusions. Since we all differ in how we perceive and judge, then we differ in how we relate to the world around us. The MBTI mirror or instrument views through four lenses as follows.

Extrovert or **I**ntrovert
  - Do you relate more to the external or internal world?

Sensing or i**N**tuition
  - How do you prefer to take in or perceive information?

Thinking or **F**eeling
  - How do you prefer to make conclusions and decisions?

Judging or **P**erceiving
  - Do you seek organization and closure or are you open and spontaneous?

With two possibilities for each of the four preferences, this gives us sixteen MBTI types. For example, an INTP person prefers **I**ntroversion, i**N**tuition, **T**hinking and **P**erceiving. The MBTI theory believes that we are born with a natural pre-disposition to four of the eight traits. We develop these preferred traits in early life and this gives us a particular personality. In later life and with knowledge, we can also develop and strengthen the weaker traits to be more balanced as needed. For example, an extrovert like myself will deliberately schedule and seek more alone, reflective time to develop and leverage my less dominant introverted side.

As with the Enneagram, there is no right or wrong MBTI type, there is no better or worse type. There is, however, knowledge and understanding. Reliable and trustworthy instruments like Myers Briggs can help you understand the terrain with a good map so you can navigate work and life more successfully. I, for, example am an ESTJ and this helps me know my preferences and when to deploy them and when not. And of course, this helps me work my traps.

Again, the same uncle who introduced me to the Enneagram in 1985 introduced me to Myers Briggs. I am forever grateful to him for this and so much more.

As with the friendly warning issued above with the Enneagram, please do not assume you know what MBTI type someone else is and please do not judge someone even if you do. I feel confident to share my MBTI and Enneagram type, because even if others judge me armed with this information, they still cannot really know where each of my actions is coming from. Heck, sometimes I do not even know myself! I meet people who have insights into these models and they judge and label people, and this is very regrettable.

I am very conscious that I have given far less detail with Myers Briggs than I did with the Enneagram, and maybe in a later edition of this handbook I will redress this, but in the interim you can find more information on this wonderful model on the website of the Myers & Briggs Foundation http://www.myersbriggs.org/.

Summary of Know your Personality

To be an effective leader of others, you need to first know yourself and be self-aware. This chapter has made much of the Enneagram, as this is the model that I encountered that helped me the most. However, the real point of the chapter is not the Enneagram, rather it is personality models and their utility. To be self-aware you can invest in strong mirrors like the Enneagram, Myers Briggs or other models you encounter, and you will get significant benefit. I hope you make space in your schedule from time to time, to learn and benefit from such models. I hope you get to know yourself better, so you can indeed lead from the inside out.

Let me conclude this chapter with a very insightful quote from Isabel Briggs Myers: *"When people differ, a knowledge of type lessens friction and eases strain. In addition, it reveals the value of differences. No one has to be good at everything."*

Questions for a "Personality" REP

Where do you now stand on the link between Personality types and successful Personal and Collaborative Leadership?

Start: When you are ready or feel the need to REP this area, do some research and select a personality model to work with (or just start with the Enneagram). Get to know yourself more deeply and make decisions on what to make use of (e.g. your strengths) and where to make adjustments (e.g. your traps).

Evolve: Rinse, lather, and repeat with the first model you selected! Later explore and move to a new model (e.g. MBTI). When you are ready, bring these models to your friends and to your team at work.

Manage Your Time (A Five Step Approach)

Introduction

Time is a finite resource that we all wish we could top up every now and then! Juggling multiple, and sometimes competing, professional and personal commitments makes effective time management seem almost impossible. However, it is important to take control and manage your time, so that you can live and lead your life with intention.

Motivation: Why Manage Your Time?

When I think of effective time management, I am reminded of the last two lines of Mary Oliver's wonderful poem, "The Summer Day":

> *"Tell me, what is it you plan to do with your one wild*
> *and precious life?"*

Two thoughts about this quote:

- for me, it sums up a key motivation for this time management chapter really well
- when you get some quiet time you might reflect personally on this profound question.

The Essence

This chapter advocates a simple and systematic 5-step approach to time management as follows:

- Step 1: Set your goals both personal and professional.
- Step 2: Create a generic schedule for how you want the typical week to progress.
- Step 3: Take time out every week to plan the coming week ahead of you so the work happens on purpose and not by accident.

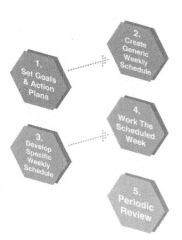

- Step 4: Work your week as you planned and make use of the 3 D's (Decide-Delegate-Defer) when handling and managing the inevitable distractions.
- Step 5: Take time out to do a periodic review a few times a year to reflect, recalibrate and reset.

Time Out

As we start into this chapter here are a few questions for you to consider:

- How effective is your time management?
- What's good about it?
- What's not so good?
- What do you think is missing?

Step 1: Set Goals and Action Plans

A goal is something you aim for that will have value to you once achieved or maybe partially achieved. A goal will lead you to a desired outcome that you call out and reach for. Goals can be personal or professional or a mix of both. A goal typically requires some degree of effort from you and maybe others helping along the way. Goals typically have deadlines, and this helps with prioritization. Goals need to be somehow attainable, even if you are not sure how. You also need to know how to judge when the goals is reached. Other names for goal, include objective and target. When you set a goal it helps chart a course for you to follow. It gives you direction.

> *"If one does not know to which port one is sailing, no wind is favorable." – Lucius Annaeus Seneca (Roman Philosopher, Statesman and Satirist: about 4 BC to AD 65)*

In Step 1 of this five step approach you set your goals and draw up any action plans needed. This first step is divided into two sub-steps, as simple as A and B!

- Step 1A: Devise your personal and professional goals and commit them to paper
- Step 1B: Devise any necessary action plans.

Step 1A: Devise Your Goals

Step 1A in this simple approach is to devise your goals. Now I know that this is easier said than done, so you are going to need to take some time to do this. If you do not devise your goals right now, you can do so on another pass through this handbook. The goals can be personal, professional, work related, anything you desire. The goals can be near, medium or long term. It does not matter as long as these are the goals that are important to you.

What would you say are the goals for the life you are currently leading? Moreover, more importantly – what are the goals for the life you wish to lead? Big questions, I know!

The question then becomes – how do you achieve these goals? The first suggestion is to verbalize your goals. In other words, share your goals, or some of them, with somebody, and go public to some degree with them. If you do this, I find that you are also more likely to achieve whatever goals it is you want to achieve. Maybe it is an ego thing! If the people you tell care for you, they will ask every now and again how these goals are progressing. They hold you accountable without really knowing it!

I have found also that it is important to write down my goals. The very act of first dreaming about and thinking out my goals and then committing them to paper has always helped me increase the likelihood of attaining my goals.

The ideal output of Step 1 is a written goal sheet. This sheet will have goals that are important to you, and these will be different to those of your friend, your neighbor, your brother, your sister. These are your goals. Of course the goals will evolve so do not be in any way nervous about your initial decisions and remember that it is important to start somewhere.

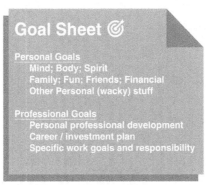

Goal Sheet

Personal Goals
   Mind; Body; Spirit
   Family; Fun; Friends; Financial
   Other Personal (wacky) stuff

Professional Goals
   Personal professional development
   Career / investment plan
   Specific work goals and responsibility

On the image above, you will see a suggested list of categories, but if they are not all helpful, ignore them. This sample should give you a sense of the variety of goals that you may have on your sheet.

I started doing this formally back in 1990 on a file-o-fax, where there was a section in the back for goals. I am still doing it today and I believe that I will be doing it for a long time to come! Today I have six main life goals – a mixture of personal and professional. These days I use Microsoft OneNote to capture my goals and the changes to them. In the extract below from my personal OneNote folder (showing the dates of the main revisions), you see my recent goal sheets started in 2005.

You can also see from the next extract below that in 2017, I made many revisions to my goal sheet. There was an amazing amount of stuff happening, mostly good with a lot of new opportunity, so my goals needed revision. Second, formally putting these Time Management materials together for the next edition of this handbook required me to really think through my goals yet again! I sharpened my own personal approach to goal management because of this sharing. A happy accident.

In summary, Step 1A – have a goal sheet. Write your goals down in a place where you can easily access them so you can live by them, and as time goes on, revise them. This is arguably the most important and maybe the least implemented step in time management – actually deciding how you want to spend your time. If you have the time right now, I suggest you devise and write down your goals. What do you wish to do with your precious time?

A Perspective on Goals

Bill, a very dear friend and mentor of mine, read the first edition of the handbook and gave the following feedback that I thought was well worth including.

"Long (or even medium) term goals have never been much of a factor in my own success. Three things that I now regularly share as planning and mentoring advice are:

– *First, work very hard to accomplish something significant and important to you every month, and thus be able to describe at least ten meaningful things you achieved at the end of the year. Failing two months out of twelve is no big deal.*

– *Second, always remember the Pareto principle, sometimes referred to as the 80-20 rule. In every situation, there are really only a few factors or items that really matter and those are what you need to identify and spend your time on.*

– *And third, what separates the really high achievers from the pack is deep personal drive and responsibility – forcing yourself to go the extra mile even when you may be worn out, stressed, angry, etc.*

Lastly, in my own experience, the single most important factor influencing project success is project size. Most organizations err in making the project too big and tackling too much at once; addressing this challenge is something you may want to focus on. The key is to pick a couple of important items (the Pareto principle at work again) and then break them down into pieces, so you can get something meaningful done in a duration of just a month or two."

Step 1B: Devise Action Plans

There are three ways to think about your goals. Some goals are so simple that it is obvious what you have to do once you write them down, and in these cases the goals do not require an action plan.

Some goals are more involved but if they are part of a business plan or a project plan, this action planning is already done!

The middle ground is where you have goals that you have set which do require an action plan. With an action plan, you know what is to happen and when it has to happen. The path to the success of your goal is more certain. It is therefore advisable that in the same place as you have written your goals, you write any necessary action plans that do not exist elsewhere.

Plans are just that – plans! Life rarely goes to plan as we know, but it is important to have a plan to chart a course. Later steps in this five step approach to time management will suggest you revisit and revise these action plans as needed.

Step 2: Create a Generic Schedule for Your Working Week

Step 2 suggests you create a generic schedule for your typical working week. This step also has two elements:
- Step 2A: Create a Generic Schedule
- Step 2B: Create a Plan Week Approach

Step 2A: Create a Generic Schedule

Step 2A suggests that you create a generic or typical schedule for your working week. All of this generic schedule will not apply to every week, e.g. during a vacation week you will want to do something radically different. You also know if you are on a training course or attending a conference or out for company meetings that only some of this generic schedule will apply.

For the typical week, what is your generic schedule? You start creating your generic schedule by going back to look at your goals (devised in Step 1). As you look at all your goals, you realize that they cannot happen by accident. You have to allocate time to achieve these goals.

What you need to do is block out specific times for the achievement of specific goals. Perhaps use different colors for the different goal/time blocks. In my case, green time on my calendar represents personal goal time; a nice shade of red represents time slots for Customer Success goals, and so on. Think back to when you were in school and you had a timetable set for you! Here you are developing the equivalent for your more mature life. I use Microsoft Outlook to create recurring blocks for major goals similar to the way you might have a recurring appointment in your calendar for a regular team meeting.

Look at the entire week from when you wake until you sleep, and decide how much you want to allocate to the achievement of your goals, mindful of the fact that you are never going to be able to stick to this exactly, so do not worry about getting it wrong. I will come back to this point later.

If relaxation, downtime, and having fun is a goal, then you will naturally allocate time to these critical activities as part of this step, but if these are not formal goals, do leave white space for same.

Of course, in a work and project management context, you are going to have project and team meetings, so you need to overlay your work and project commitments on to this generic calendar.

By using this approach, you are saying, "I live my life one week at a time, one day at a time, and one time block at a time". You are devising how you are going to use the typical week to achieve your specific goals and live the life that you desire, the life you deserve.

Example: Microsoft Outlook

Here is an example of a schedule derived from my own calendar. There are some personal goal-times and some work goals here with specific times set aside for items like e-mail and to-do lists, all of which are important but you do not want them to take over your schedule. We talk about this in the next chapter on "Manage Your Time – Eighteen Traps and Tips".

You can see that certain goals translate into designated spaces on the calendar. You can also see white space. As you start a week with white space, identify which goals slot into this available time.

You can also see that I have time set aside every week to REP – actually the very first part of my week. As it happens I still love my job and am happy going to work each day, but knowing that my first session on a Monday morning is REP (where I invest in my professional and personal development) makes it even easier. This sample extract only shows Monday, Tuesday and Wednesday. If you could see Sunday, you would see an early morning time slot where I have extra time set aside to enjoy a REP for my personal development.

Your personal and professional development is important on so many fronts, but it will not happen by accident. Set regular time aside each week and make it happen. Do not short change yourself. Make the most of your time by striving to achieve your goals, by allocating the time. Make the time investment.

In all of this, you are striving to map your key goals to the available time whilst also trying to create routine. You are certainly not trying to be boring. However, there is a sense with routine that is empowering, that is enabling, that makes it easier for you to just focus on what you are meant to do at that point in time and to produce higher quality work that you are more satisfied with. A schedule like this can really help you live in the moment and enjoy the present, while knowing that your future is planned.

Work Life Balance

This simple but systematic five step approach to time management encourages you to make a decision on how much time you give to each major area of your life, and as such helps you be intentional about how you use your time. How many hours per week will you give to work, career, family, friends, hobbies, etc.? Simple but very important questions are asked and answered in how you approach this thought process.

It is important to have a work life balance. "All work and no play makes Jack a dull boy", is very true. I do however have an issue with how some people characterize the work life divide. They often characterize 'work' as drudge, less worthy of our time than 'life' and something to be minimized in this 'balance'. Work should be enjoyable, challenging, fulfilling and rewarding. Work should be a social outlet where companionship and support is found. Surely, this type of work is also life! In the prior chapter on 'Manage Your Energy' we talked about Career and Work Choices.

How you approach this question will determine how much time you give to work each week. These days, because of my current goals, I willingly give 60+ hours to 'work' each week at this juncture of my life. I will add that careful attention to Time Management and the other practices in this handbook help me be happy with what is achieved inside and outside of these 60+ hours. I know some people will think this is insane, but the key to remember, is that this is my conscious choice for now.

In addition to the above, I often hear people use the work life balance discussion as an excuse to do less work. There are times when you will have ambitious goals that you want to achieve and you need to give this part of your life more time. There are times when you family and friends really need you and you need to give this part of your life more time. Don't worry if you get out of balance from time to time. This is feedback that you have might have found your current limits. And, how are you going to know your limits unless you cross them.

You will benefit from deciding the typical or generic balance that you give to each major area of your life. This is a personal decision you make and will revise from time to time.

Step 2B: Create a Plan Week Approach

In Step 2A, we suggested creating a generic schedule for your typical week. In Step 2B, we recommend you devise a simple process to actually plan your week. Now why would you do something like this?! Well, if you think about it, a week is an amazing amount of time. Each week is a new gift. There is a huge amount of time in a week if you just approach it the right way.

Example: Plan Week Approach

Here, you can see a simple process that will give you some sense of what you might do in the time slot called, 'Plan Week.' This example extracted from my personal approach and it has five simple steps as depicted in the next image. These repeatable steps prompt me to make the best use of the week ahead.

Management

Subject	Plan Week
Location	
Recurrence	Occurs every Monday effective 29th July 2002 from 11:30 to 12:30

Schedule time for:

- Eamonn personal goals achievement
- Any already scheduled meetings (e.g. webcasts, project meetings) that need prep
- Business Plan - Strategic Deliverables
- Quarterly Strategy Review or Annual Business Planning
- Re-schedule any follow-up tasks on the calendar

In the first step, I look at my personal and professional goals to see which of my goals need progress this week and where can I fit them in. Sometimes the time is already allocated on my generic schedule, so it is a case of re-affirming my commitment to this slot and often deciding exactly what I will do with this time. Other times, I will need to use the available white space to allocate to these goals. Looking at these goals once a week like this, I now re-assess how I am doing and I commit to doing the same or better this coming week. We need to be happy with our personal goal achievement and this weekly check is important and helpful in this regard.

Second of my steps is to look at any pre-ordained meetings in the coming week. Typically, I will have many meetings in an average week and I have a passionate dislike for meetings that are a waste of time, as I am sure you do too. This means I have to prepare for these meetings. I look at the scheduled meetings and decide if I need to do prep. If so, I will allocate the preparation time, usually just before the meeting if I can. If it is not possible to prepare properly, I will try to reschedule the meeting to save wasting everybody else's time and mine. For some recurring meetings I have prep time scheduled on my generic calendar.

Third step is I, like you, am involved in many projects. I will look at these specific plans and see what items need to happen this week to keep that business or these projects on track. Typically, I will allocate these items to whatever white space I can find.

At certain times of the year, I will have a fourth step in my weekly schedule planning. This will entail setting time aside to work on business planning or other business or major project reviews.

My fifth, and final, step in the typical week is to look at my to-do list, my task list, my overflow. You will see in the approach we are going to recommend in the next chapter that you do not action every item when it comes up; instead, you will put some of these items on a to-do list. However, these to-do's will not get done by accident! In this fifth step, I look at my tasks list, which is important, but typically not as important as the other goals and projects in Steps 1, 2, 3 of this weekly planning template. I will allocate time to the bigger tasks that need to get done this week.

The steps described above are my generic planning process for the specific week that I have in front of me. Your planning steps will likely differ, but hopefully the above will give you some ideas.

Step 3: Develop the Specific Schedule (for this week)

In Step 3, develop a specific schedule for the week you now have in front of you. If you think of the prior steps 1 and 2, they can be summarized as follows:

- Step 1 is **devise your goals** (and you do this every now and again – not every day!).
- Step 2 is **develop the generic template** for how you are going to organize your time.

I treat each new week as a fresh start, and I also see a week as a large chunk of time. Step 3 advocates that as each new week starts, you take time to have that meeting with yourself to decide how you are going to spend this coming week.

When do you do this? I will typically do this on Monday just before lunch. I used to do this planning on Monday morning very first thing but not anymore. I have found it is best to do the most difficult and important work first thing in the morning instead of emails or time planning like this Step 3.

Sometimes I get overwhelmed with too much work – most often when I forget to say "No" to new opportunities! Maybe you also find that sometimes there is too much going on and you wonder how you are going to get through everything.

Being overwhelmed can often come because you have too much on your plate. We need to remember there are only so many hours in the day and only so many days in the week. By planning your week, you are saying, 'This is what I am going to get done and this will have to wait' and, 'I know when I am going to defer this to'. This approach can relax you so you can enjoy the rest of your day, week or weekend.

In these times of overwhelm, on a Friday before I leave work or sometimes over the weekend, I will sneak away for an hour or less to plan the week ahead to figure the best way through and thereby clear my head.

The key in Step 3 is that you have a pre-set allocated time for this plan-your-week activity. In fact, if you looked closely at the image above and partially repeated here, you will see that this Microsoft Outlook calendar entry for me that started in 2002.

Subject	Plan Week
Location	Meeting Room A
Recurrence	Occurs every Monday effective 29th July 2002 from 11:30 to 12:30

Back in 2002, I started using Microsoft Outlook to schedule this meeting with myself to plan how I am going to get the most out of my week. This is a simple but helpful practice that has worked well for me and I am happy to recommend it to you.

When planning your week, I would also suggest that you are very realistic. Do not think you can get ten things done if you are only going to get five done. This judgement will come with practice but be realistic from the outset. Also, set enough time aside so whatever you are doing, you can do well and to a standard that you and your colleagues are happy with.

Finally, as you plan your specific weeks, bear in mind that the schedule will not work out exactly as you had planned – it will change – so assume changes. Your schedule will be more realistic, even relaxing, and you will be more successful and happier.

Step 4: Work the Schedule/Plan

Step 4 is where you work the plan and spend the time planned. In the first 3 steps of this approach you have put time into defining your goals, your generic schedule and your specific schedule, so whatever you are doing right now is what you have decided you want to do. You should be able to relax and enjoy doing it, because you know that you are going to get to the other priorities later. Ironically, some people think that a schedule is restrictive but planning your week like this is liberating and should actually help you live in the moment and be present in the now.

You are probably now asking the following questions. What about changes? What about distractions? What about interruptions? It is all very well to live in the moment and be relaxed but when I get distracted, when somebody walks up with something different, when I get interrupted, when the plan does not go the way I want, what do I do?

Distraction is a reality and many times, can be a real gift, so we need mechanisms and space to deal with this reality. My mother reminds me that *"life is something that happens when you are planning something else!"*

The next chapter in this handbook is "Manage Your Time – Eighteen Traps and Tips". In this next chapter, I talk through eighteen traps that suck away at your time and eighteen tips to deal with them.

In the next section of the current chapter, I will give you one helpful technique to get you started.

Managing Distractions

Managing distractions – yikes! I have observed that the people who are very easily distracted and often interrupted are people who do not set goals and do not have their schedules organized. They are not living their life in a purposeful way. That may be a bit harsh and does not take into account some roles that are, by their very nature, prone to interruption, but you can observe yourself and see if this aligns with your experiences. I find that the best defense against being randomized by others is to first get myself organized.

As promised, let me give you one technique to get you started. When a distraction comes that is trying to take you away from what you should be doing right now on your schedule, remember these 3 D's – "Decide-Delegate-Defer".

Decide

The first D is **make a decision**. This should be the first priority. When a distraction arises, you decide if you want to take this distraction or not.

If you decide you want to take it, consider: do I have to do it now, or can I do it later? If you decide to do it now, then go do it and reschedule whatever you are doing when you got distracted. The first order of march is to make a decision. You need to be the person who decides how to spend your time – not someone else.

Now I meet many people, sometimes very busy and accomplished people, and they get overwhelmed. As I mentioned earlier I get overwhelmed from time to time. It happens to all of us. In fact, in some ways this is a good sign because you are taking on lots of stuff, but we need mechanisms to cope with overwhelm and "Decide" is one simple process to deal with too much work.

Delegate

If you decide to take on the extra work that just arrived, the second D is to ask yourself can or **should I delegate it?** Now I do not mean dump it on somebody else. That is unfair.

Some people are very good at shifting work to other people who have already too much on their plate. You will also find some personality types cannot say "No" to the extra work, so be careful not to overload these good people.

Be a responsible delegator. Find somebody who can help you out with the extra work and delegate responsibly. Make sure these people are able to do the work and ensure they have the necessary support from you. Effective delegation is an active not a passive process. Think before you delegate.

Defer

The third D is **defer**. If it is important that you get the extra item done, maybe it does not have to be done right now? If it is important but not urgent, can you defer to another time?

Allocate this extra item to a specific time slot on your calendar or add the item to a to-do/task list. In the meantime, you can get back to whatever you should be doing right now, finish that out, and enjoy doing your current work.

In summary to help with distractions, remember the 3 D's –

Decide, Delegate, Defer. Of course, as you traverse the 3 Ds at any stage you may indeed decide to Do the action (the 4th D!).

Side Note: I view email as very useful and necessary but also as a potential and special type of distraction. As such, the least two chapters in this section 2 give steps to help manage email well.

Step 5: Periodic Review

If you look back at the process and approach we have worked so far, steps 3 and 4 involve a natural amount of continuous review. These reviews, while important, can tend to be more microscopic rather than macroscopic, if you get my drift. Every now and again it is important to get back to Steps 1 and 2 and ask yourself some hard questions, e.g.,

- The '3H' (happy, healthy, helpful) questions:
  - Am I happy?
  - Am I healthy?
  - Am I helpful to others?

- The 'life potential' questions:
  - Am I successful with my goals? (whatever success means to you personally)
  - Am I living to my full potential?
  - Am I the best that I can be for myself and people who are important to me?

Step 5 is about setting time aside to review how you are doing against your personal and professional goals. It is honestly acknowledging that you are not going to give yourself an A+ grade on your goal and time management the first time around. It is just not going to happen! Moreover, life changes anyway, so periodically there are going to be natural adjustments that need to take place.

If you think about it, it takes time to learn how to ride a bike, to swim, to horse-ride, to play golf, to become a marketer, an engineer, etc. Whatever it is that you are good at, it has taken time. Recent wisdom tells us that it can take ten thousand hours of practice to achieve personal mastery in some areas, so you better get started soon with time management!

Therefore, with Step 5 you take some time out and relook at the goals identified in Step 1. Assess your energy levels. Examine how you allocated your generic week in Step 2 and decide if you want to make some adjustments. I aim to do this at least once a year but sometimes I review more than this. This review typically happens around significant dates such as the start of the year or when I get back from summer vacation. Whenever it triggers for you, go with that process and make the adjustments.

There is another point to make here. What I am really saying to you is be intentional, decide the life you want to lead and do not drift for too much or for too long. While you will want to be spontaneous, I am also suggesting that you have personal and professional goals to guide and live the life that you want. Now, this readjustment should not be stressful. This periodic review should actually be enjoyable because it is like a reboot, a restart, and a chance to go again.

Remember that 'practice makes perfect' in all endeavors. It will take time to be good at time management, so how do you expect to get it perfect on your first attempt? You can't. You shouldn't. This periodic review is your chance to improve your time management, and you need to take advantage of and enjoy this reflection.

Summary of Time Management – a Five Step Approach

This chapter started with the last two lines of a Mary Oliver poem:

"Tell me, what is it you plan to do with your one wild and precious life?"

Food for thought! A big question really worth answering for yourself, if you did not do so as we started this chapter.

In summary, this chapter recommends the following five steps:

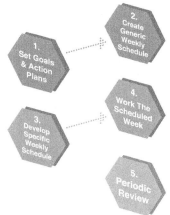

- Step 1: Set your goals both personal and professional.
- Step 2: Create a generic schedule for how you want

the typical week to progress.

- Step 3: Take time out every week to plan the week ahead of you, so it happens on purpose and not by accident.
- Step 4: Work your week as you planned and remember the 3 D's (Decide-Delegate-Defer) when handling and managing the inevitable distractions.
- Step 5: Take time out to do a periodic review once or twice a year to reflect, recalibrate and reset. Moreover, enjoy this step, and get renewed energy from this review.

Questions for a "Time Management" REP

Start: Spend some time working on your goals when you are ready or feel the need to REP this area. (If your goals are sharply in focus, you will naturally begin to make better use of time.)

Evolve: Start working through some of the other suggestions in this approach to help reach your goals and make better use of your time.

Manage Your Time (Eighteen Traps and Tips)

Introduction

There is a wonderful quote from Benjamin Franklin:

> *"Dost thou love life? Then do not squander time, for that is*
> *the stuff that life is made of."*

Feel free to set down this handbook for a few minutes to think about this quote and what it means for you, because in many ways it sums up the motivation for this chapter.

Motivation: Why Eighteen Traps and Tips?

Welcome back if you enjoyed a time-out! This chapter will walk you through traps and tips in these three areas:

- Your goals
- Your schedule
- The inevitable distractions.

The chapter calls out the traps you might fall into and suggests tips to avoid these obstacles. Eighteen traps and tips in all.

The Essence

The main message of this chapter is as follows: if you knew that the road you were driving was full of holes, you would avoid the holes! It is wise to know where the time management traps are and avoid them!

Time Out

As we start this chapter, reflect on the traps and distractions that currently trip you up, that make you feel, 'Ugh, I did not get as much done today as I should have done.' What are these traps? Having written your thoughts, I suggest another
question. "How do you think you could avoid these traps? How could you make them less distracting, less distressing?"

Goals: Five Traps and Tips

We are going to start with Goals – no surprises there. Those who read the last chapter (Manage Your Time – a Five Step Approach) will know that I have a strong bias for being very clear on your personal and professional goals.

What I often find is that people who become disappointed or overwhelmed are typically not achieving their goals, stated or unstated, personal or professional. This may not come to the fore. It may not be what people are thinking consciously, but deeper down this is what is often being felt.

This particular section is going to walk you through five traps and tips to make sure you are on track to achieve your goals because I believe that this will really set you up for fulfilment, contentment, success and happiness.

Goals Trap No. 1: Not Achieving Your Goals

Trap: Do you feel as though you are spending the time and not achieving your goals? This can be very frustrating.

Tip: Have you a written set of goals? If not, consider writing your goals in simple, clear, unambiguous, and achievable terms. If you do have written goals, then go back to them. Relook at them and re-evaluate them. Maybe they are the wrong goals. Alternatively, maybe you just need to refocus on them. (Refer to Step 1 in the "Manage Your Time – a Five Step Approach" chapter if you need more guidance.)

Goals Trap No. 2: Unclear Path to Success

Trap: Are some of your goals a bit fuzzy? Perhaps you have a very clear goal but you are not quite sure how to achieve it? You know what you want, you know the desired end-state, but you are not yet on a clear path to success. This can also be a huge waste of time and quite frustrating.

Tip: Go back and create a clear, concise set of actions that are time-based detailing how you will achieve each important goal. Do this, and make it no more than a page in length if you can to begin with. Take your time and do this well. Revise it from time to time as needs be.

Goals Trap No. 3: Not Getting to Your Goals

Trap: Do you feel as though you have some very important goals but you are not getting to them? This trap is quite common, because less important stuff and seemingly more urgent items gets in the way.

Tip: Come in every morning of each workday and give the first two hours to your most important goal. Now if you do not think that is a good idea, try it for a week or ideally for a month. Two hours of every day.

When you come in to work, do not even turn on your computer and if you have to, then do not look at your email. Two hours every day to achieve your most important goal; you will make amazing progress in a few weeks and months. You will be well on the road. I "cheat" a small bit on this one in that I do critical email and time-sensitive tasks from home before I get to work – so that when I arrive at the office my two hours start clean.

Later in this chapter, the focus will turn to distractions, but suffice it to say, that you will need to learn to say "No" or "Not Yet" or "Later" to some incoming requests, in order to keep your focus on your most important goals.

Goals Trap No. 4: Feeling Overwhelmed

Trap: Do you feel overwhelmed? This might be a reward for your success because you are taking on too much, and if so, congratulations!

Tip: It is natural and normal to be overwhelmed from time to time. If you are very overwhelmed, then you may need to schedule some down time. Just get away from it, relax, recharge, and come back refreshed. With this new energy, you can then re-organize and regain control. Even a short getaway will make a difference.

Goals Trap No. 5: Stressed

Trap: Are you stressed?

Tip: We all get stressed from time to time. It is one of the most natural feelings in the world. Try not to worry too much about it, but definitely do acknowledge stress. I know this is hard but do try. Once you acknowledge and admit you are stressed, you can now do something about it. One suggestion is to ask for help from family, friends, work colleagues, or ideally your manager, because you are in it together or you should be.

If possible, ask your manager for some advice and coaching on how to deal with work stress. If you do not feel that you can ask your manager for advice in stressful situations, as you are not confident or comfortable, ask a colleague for some advice as a starting point. Of course, if there is a larger issue with your manager that is causing unfair or unwarranted stress, you may need to work for a different manager. Food for thought.

Now is also a good time to think about your physical and emotional energy levels, as covered in the earlier chapter, 'Manage Your Energy (Ten Factors)'. If you feel physically and emotionally drained this will seriously affect your ability to manage stress.

Above you have five common time management traps and five tips, and again, this chapter started with traps and tips related to goals. I believe when you achieve clarity on your goals, a lot of the rest will begin to take care of itself, in terms of more effectively and efficiently managing your time.

Schedule: Six Traps and Tips

In the last section, I wrote about how to focus on your goals to be more effective. In this segment, I am going to address six typical time management traps and tips associated with your schedule.

Once you have sorted your goals, these need to spill into your schedule. The question now becomes: how do you make the most of your schedule? What is the most effective way? What traps do you have to avoid?

Schedule Trap No. 1: The small stuff is getting in the way

Trap: Do you find that you are getting lots of small stuff done but nothing major achieved? Do you find that you are not making progress on the more challenging items on your list?

Tip: Do Creative Work in Larger Blocks. Think about the creative work you have to do and execute this in larger blocks. Do not do this creative work in interrupted time. Schedule sixty / ninety minutes and do this creative work in a contiguous block. Ideally, do it earlier in the day before your head is swamped with too many other things.

Schedule Trap No. 2: Meetings are killing my schedule

Trap: Do you find that lots of time and energy is wasted in meetings?

Tip: Have meetings later in the day (unless the matter is urgent and delaying the meeting would cause stress). Meetings tend to have an energy all of their own, hopefully good energy, but not always the case I admit! If the meeting has good energy, then you will be carried by it.

As the day goes on and you are a little bit more tired, you will hopefully pick up the energy of that meeting instead of investing more of your own.

Schedule Trap No. 3: My Desk is a Mess!

Trap: Do you find that your workspace is distracting you and does not help your productivity?

Tip: Two computer screens and a tidy desk. For productivity and a better use of your schedule, I recommend two monitors on a moveable arm or one very large screen to give you more free space on your desk. The monitor arms give you more clutter-free space on your desk, which is good for productivity.

There is so much information flying around these days, so much information to process, compare and work through that having two screens where you can look across a wider space and drag-and-drop between the two is a very helpful productivity aid.

There is no point in asking some people to keep a tidy desk but if you can at all rise to this challenge, please try for the sake of a more productive schedule!

Schedule Trap No. 4: Getting Tired

Trap: Do you find that you are getting tired at work?

Tip: Take Breaks. If you want to get more out of your schedule, stop doing work and take some breaks! At least every hour or ninety minutes, take a short break. Walk away and come back. Walk outside and take some fresh air. The suggestion is not to do four to six hours of solid work because you just will not be as productive.

There is plenty of extra advice in the earlier chapter, "Manage Your Energy (Ten Factors)", if you are feeling more tired than you believe you should be – but for now start with taking breaks away from the desk.

Schedule Trap No. 5: Creativity does not happen at my computer screen

Trap: Do you find it difficult to be inspired and get creative ideas at your desk?

Tip: Get away from your desk! If you have creative work to do such as reviewing a document or creating a new strategy, then get away from your desk and your computer. Find a space that is creative for you.

I have quite an old chair that the office-design folks would prefer to remove from our office, but it is still very comfortable. I sit in that chair with a document or a notepad to get away from my desk and do some of my creative thinking there, even though it is only three feet away! Similarly at home, I have a go to space in which I find it easier to be creative. This space works for me. Have you a favorite creative space?

Schedule Trap No. 6: Disconnected from my colleagues

Trap: Do you find that you are not always sure what is happening with the team? Do you find that priorities change and you are not always told? Do you waste time as a result? This can be frustrating.

Tip: Invest in productive team meetings at least once a week. For example, many teams I work with do a daily stand-up for ten minutes or so and a more formal meeting once a week using a pre-set agenda. These sessions are great team communications and they save a lot of time on the back-and-forth throughout the week.

These are six traps and associated tips to take into consideration to help you make the best use of your schedule all day every day.

Distractions: Seven Traps and Tips

In this section, I am going to talk about the inevitable distractions and interruptions that eat away at your time. I will walk you through seven of the most common traps that distract you from a productive schedule. I will also give you seven tips to help minimize these distractions.

Distractions Trap No. 1: I Am So Connected

Trap: I know it sounds like a blessing that you are always connected via email, social media, text messages, and mobile phones but this is also a major trap! It is so easy for others to interrupt you, even if this is not the best thing for you right now.

Tip: Set aside specific times of the day when you will manage your email, phone messages and your social media, for example, in a short slot before lunch and perhaps in the hour before you leave in the evening.

There are many obvious advantages to this practice, the main one being that your communications are much more effective and enjoyable because you are not snatching at emails quickly. You are now saying, 'For this hour, I am doing emails and my other communications. I will do them well and enjoy doing them and I am not feeling guilty because I should be working something important.'

Distractions Trap No. 2: Email

Trap: It is amazing how much time we lose by managing email poorly.

Tip: Develop a systematic, but simple way, to manage your email. Do not just "do email". If you do not have an approach, the next chapter ("Save Time – Manage Your Email (Six Tips)") will give you a simple process to consider.

Distractions Trap No. 3: The Random Thought

Trap: It is a real gift to have a flow of fabulous ideas. The time trap is dropping what you are doing to research and action every idea when it comes. Before you know it, you are all over the place!

Tip: To overcome this trap, have a simple place to write down these ideas. For example, I use a combination of Microsoft OneNote and Microsoft Outlook Tasks. With Outlook I create a task scheduled for action at some day in the future and come back to it at that point to play with the idea in a more relaxed way.

Distractions Trap No. 4: The To-Do list

Trap: We absolutely need the to-do list. It is a vital asset in our time management toolbox. The trap is letting your to-do list become your daily work and the main priority. Sometimes you do this because it is easier to do, but in this scenario, you are not achieving what you really need to achieve.

Tip: Have a daily slot allocated for your to-do list. Pick off a few items, get them done, typically later in the day, and then happily mark them off one-by-one.

You can, of course, steal minutes and hours throughout the day where you can get these smaller and often important to-dos' completed. You call your mother as you drive to work. You finish a chunk of larger work earlier than expected (maybe because you focus on it and it alone!) and you then do a few smaller but important items from your to-do list before you start your next scheduled major item of work.

Distractions Trap No. 5: I Can Multi-Task

Trap: Another big trap: multi-tasking! I wager when you measure the time taken to do three things at once, you will find if takes longer than if you did one after the other in sequence and with more focus. Moreover, sustained multi-tasking is more stressful.

Tip: Pick 15/30/60/90 minutes to do one thing really well instead of stressing yourself trying to do five things at once. It is good to have the multi-tasking skill, but use it when you have to and not as a default, as this can be a real time trap.

Distractions Trap No. 6: Open Office Communication

Trap: I work in a fabulous, wonderfully designed modern open office. However, it can be a trap when people come up and they think, 'Oh it is so easy to get to Eamonn, let me ask him now'.

Tip: Develop some protocol for working in the open office, so you do not get constantly distracted. You want to encourage communication and collaboration, but you might say to these people, "Jack, I am looking forward to talking to you about this; let me finish what I am doing and I will come back to you later". Nine times out of ten, this will be just fine. Every now and again, it will be urgent for that person to meet sooner and of course, you will need to accommodate this.

Distractions Trap No. 7: Your Personal Time Waster (e.g. Time "TV Channel / Internet Surfing")

Trap: Most of us do something that is a complete waste of time! Mine is (or used to be) to surf through the TV channels looking for something better to watch! What is yours? Maybe it is spending too much time online? Take this example – if I were to spend 15 minutes of unproductive / unenjoyable time TV channel surfing every day, then by my calculations this is the equivalent of three years of my working life! Now that is a lot of time wasted!

Time TV Channel / Internet Surfing	
	15 minutes / day
7 days in a week	105 minutes / week
52 weeks in a year	5,460 minutes / year
60 years in the adult life	327,600 minutes / adult life
60 minutes in an hour	5,460 hours / adult life
39 hours in a working week	140 weeks / adult life
46 weeks in a working year	3 years / adult life

Tip: Figure out what your vice is. What wastes your time? What takes away your energy? Figure how many minutes it sucks from you each day and do the math. This calculation might help you stop or at least cut down!

Above, my friends, are seven traps and tips to help you manage the inevitable distractions that eat away at your time.

Summary of 'Manage Your Time – Traps and Tricks'

We started this chapter with a quote from Benjamin Franklin:

"Dost thou love life?"

And of course the assumed answer is: you do. Then the quote went on to say:

Then do not squander time, for that is the stuff that life
is made of."

This chapter has given you eighteen tips to overcome the many traps and distractions that get in your way of having a productive week. These distractions happen to everyone – what differentiates us is how we deal with them.

This chapter presented:
- Five tips to help you achieve your goals
- Six tips to help better manage your schedule
- Seven tips to help you work around the inevitable distractions that take away from your time.

Questions for a "Time Management" REP

Did you identify ways to deal with the inevitable traps that trip you up when trying to manage your time effectively and efficiently?

Start: Set a goal to adopt one or two of these time management tips when you are ready or feel the need to REP this area.

Evolve: Make time to return to the other tips as needed.

Save Time – Manage Your Email (Six Tips)

Introduction

We live in an incredibly connected world. At any given time, your desktop, phone, tablet, maybe your watch, might be beeping with new email notifications. However, all these emails are distracting you from what you had decided to do right now.

Motivation: Why Manage Your Email?

Did you know for every five unnecessary minutes you spend on email each day, you are tracking to lose one full work year of your life? Then double this to ten and fifteen unnecessary minutes spent on email each day. Yikes! Crazy, I know! In the image below, you can see how these calculations are made. Feel free to adjust these calculations so they are real for you.

Time Wasted on Email ✉

	5 minutes / day
7 days in a week	35 minutes / week
52 weeks in a year	1,820 minutes / year
60 years in the adult life	109,200 minutes / adult life
60 minutes in a hour	1,820 hours / adult life
39 hours in a working week	47 weeks / adult life
46 weeks in a work year	1 year / adult life

The Essence

This chapter will give you six tips to help you manage email more effectively and the next chapter gives four tips to help you better use Microsoft Outlook to save time. The main message of these two chapters is as follows: If you manage email more effectively and more efficiently then you can save and recover significant amounts of time.

Time Out

As we start this chapter, take a few minutes to yourself to ask yourself these questions:

- Does email hinder your productivity from time to time? Where is this email drain on your time?
- What do you think you can do to stop these leaks?

Email Management – Six Tips

It's amazing to think that something as productive as email can sap your productivity. In any event, here follows six tips to help you redress this and minimize the productivity drain.

Email Tip No. 1: Set Special Time Aside

You should set aside a specific time or times each day to do email – maybe just before lunch and before you finish in the evening.

Let me expand. You know the alerts that pop up every time you receive an email? You get a message in your tray or you get an alert on your screen or both. Switch them both off right now! You do not need these distractions. Whether on your phone, your PC or another device, being constantly interrupted by an email which is not relevant to what you are doing right now makes absolutely no sense – turn these off. I acknowledge that there may be some emergency situations when you need these alerts and if so turn them back on as needed.

Allied to this, do not always open your inbox. If you have your email open because you need it for work, for whatever project work you are doing, then do not have your cursor in the inbox, because waiting for all those new emails to come in will distract you from what you should be doing right now. Ideally, when you are not doing email, turn off Outlook. Do not have your email open all day, as it is a serious productivity drain.

Now if you are thinking that you need access to your email for some of your project work, I understand. In these situations, have your email open and have your cursor sit in the Drafts folder, so you can get access to the older emails without getting distracted by the stream of new emails arriving in your Inbox.

By setting a specific time aside for email, you are going to feel: "I am now doing email, I can do it in a less stressed way and I can actually enjoy doing it guilt-free. I can do it well."

Email Tip No. 2: Clear your Inbox

Clear your inbox at least once a day or at a minimum once a week. This is going to be pretty radical for some people but worth the effort. Having ten, twenty, hundreds or thousands of emails in your Inbox to search through is a complete distraction and a waste of time.

In Tip No. 6, we will give you a very systematic approach to help you manage your inbox better if you are not sure how.

Email Tip No. 3: One Archive folder and Search to Find Emails

Do not create multiple folders to store different types of emails. If you have many email folders, you will spend time trying to figure which folder to put the email in and extra time trying to find that folder.

Even worse, when you need to find an email, you will have to waste time looking through folders to find the required email. The more folders you have, the more time you waste.

Microsoft and most email systems give you a standard set of folders like Inbox, Draft, Outbox, Sent and Deleted. Keep these folders! The nice thing about these folders is emails automatically move between them. The suggestion is you create one extra folder and call it 'Archive'. Then put all the emails that you want to keep into the 'Archive' folder.

A variant on this theme is helpful if you use the same email address for work and for personal email. In this scenario you might have two Archive folders (e.g. Archive-Work and Archive-Personal). An alternative is that you setup an email address for personal stuff like credit cards, bank, flight bookings, etc.

Some emails are deleted anyway so they take care of sorting themselves. Put anything you want to keep into 'Archive' and then learn how to use 'Search' (and we will explain in the next chapter how to do this). Once you learn how to use 'Search' to manage your emails, it will save you a huge amount of time.

Email Tip No. 4: Pre-Composed Emails

If you think about it, you are probably asked some questions repeatedly. Apart from the fact that this can be frustrating, you typically do not have the time to answer well. Create an email to keep in your Drafts folder, or another folder, and take the extra time to answer those common questions very well in that one draft email.

When you are asked questions again and again, go to your Drafts folder, copy the answer and paste it into the email that you are replying to. You will then have time to contextualize it, personalize it and send off a considered answer that will really help and impress the recipient. You will also feel much better about the more considered email response you are giving to that person.

Email Tip No. 5: Do not Answer When Angry or Give Bad News

Tip No. 5 might seem like an unusual one. Do not, whatever you do, answer an email when angry and do not give bad news or very critical feedback on email.

If you receive an email that makes you boil inside, do not reply and whatever you do, please do not "reply-all". Now if you must answer the email, write an answer and save it but do not send it. Come back a day later and review it. My advice is still not to send very critical feedback on email, but if you must, review and edit it again one day later and then send it.

If you have bad news to give or very critical feedback to deliver; if there is a row you want to have or if there is some stressful situation to deal with, do not deal with it in an email. Physically go to the person and have a one-on-one private meeting or phone the person at a place where they can take the call with some privacy.

Now apart from the fact that these tips are good etiquette and a better way to treat people, no matter how they treat you, you might well ask, 'Why are these tips in a time management chapter?' The reason is if you answer emails when angry or you send bad news on email, you are going to waste more time in the long-run dealing with the fall-out, so using email in this situation is not a time-saver. In fact, it is quite the opposite. Trust me, I have made this mistake!

Email Tip No. 6: Have an Email Management Process

We get so much email that there is no way you should do email in a haphazard way. As email is something you do so often, you should have a simple process for it. Here are five options on how to process an email. You may break this down into something simpler, but this will hopefully get you started:

- Option 1: Read and Delete
  Read it once or do not, and delete. It is now gone out of your Inbox.
- Option 2: Read and File
  Read it once and file it in your Archive folder, not in one of thirty other folders. Read it, understand it, and put it away immediately into your Archive folder. Get it out of your Inbox. If you need it again, you can search for it.
- Option 3: Read, Reply and File

Read it and reply immediately. Do not leave it so that you reply later. Reply right now. Remember, you are in the zone and you have set aside an hour or so specifically to do your emails. In this system, you are not checking emails on your phone between meetings where you cannot reply properly to them and they are distracting you. Read and reply right now and then either delete the email or file it in that one Archive folder so it is gone out of your Inbox and addressed. Again, you have handled the email just once.

- Option 4: Read, Flag and File

  You read the email, and think, 'OK, I need to do something with this but I cannot respond properly today'. In this case flag the email for follow up on a future day and then file the email away in your Archive folder. Another email gone from your Inbox. Gone but not forgotten, because it is flagged!

- Option 5: Read, Quick-Reply, Flag and File

  You read it and you think, 'Oh, I need way more time for this', but the person is looking for a response, as it requires me to do some work, that you do not have time for right now. Read it, reply and say, 'I will get back to you in a day or two'. Maybe set some time expectation if you wish, but acknowledge the email, so that they know you have it and then flag it for follow up. Use Outlook or some such email client to put a flag on the email, so that it goes to a particular day in the future when you believe you will have time. Then file the email in your Archive folder. Now the email is gone out of your Inbox and the next time you think about the email is the day in which you need to respond to it. This email will not distract you every time you trip across it in your inbox.

The key here is that you only process each email once, or maximum twice in some cases. The goal is that you have an Inbox that is clear and you are not tripping over the same stuff repeatedly.

This concludes the six tips for making email a much more productive experience. I am not suggesting that you will get to every single tip tomorrow morning, but pick a few that work for you and come back a week or two later if these tips worked, and then pick a few more and gradually implement them until you get a better way to manage your inbox and your email.

Summary of 'Save Time – Manage Your Email'

The start of this chapter explained that:

"For every five unnecessary minutes each day you spend on email,
you are on track to lose one year of your work life!"

This chapter explains six tips to help you manage email more effectively and the next chapter gives four tips to help you better use Microsoft Outlook (or some such similar email software). These tips will help you save five or more minutes wasted on email every day, so you can save a year of your working life!

Questions for an "email Management" REP

Where do you now stand on your email management approach?

<u>Start</u>: Pick two or three practices you think will really help you use email more effectively and efficiently. Practice these when you are ready or feel the need to REP this area.

<u>Evolve</u>: Come back later to work the remaining practices.

Save Time – Microsoft Outlook (Four Tips)

This chapter explains four tips to make the best use of Microsoft Outlook (or similar email software packages) to optimize your time management. If you do not spend much time on email, this chapter will have limited appeal to you, so please do feel free to skip it. If however, you are like myself, and email is a communication mechanism you use a lot, then this chapter will probably help. Why? I see so many people use Outlook like it was 1999 and they are not taking advantage of the advances in the product.

Outlook Tip No.1: Shut it Down!

The first tip is to shut Outlook down! Close it! Turn it off! The last thing you need is to be distracted by emails all the time, so shut it off.

When you shut it off you can still use Outlook. If you look in the tray on your computer, you should see the Microsoft Outlook icon. Right-mouse-click on the icon to access a menu as you can see below.

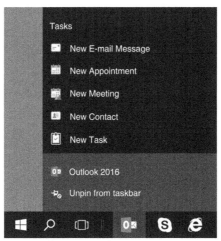

This menu will allow you to perform quick actions like writing an email or creating a task. You can still use the basic features of Outlook without ever switching it on. When you write a new email in this fashion, the email will go to your Outbox and sends once Outlook is reopened. You have now created an email or a follow-up task without ever fully starting Outlook and getting distracted by the many other emails in your inbox. Whew!

Outlook Tip No. 2: Use Flags

In the prior chapter, we talked about using flags to process email and here is an example. In my Inbox, you see that I have an email but I am not ready to deal with it now. I need to give it quality time later.

In this case I right-mouse-click on that email and a number of options appear. One of them is 'Follow Up'. I single-click on the 'Follow Up' option flag for follow up to today, tomorrow, next week, or a more specific date.

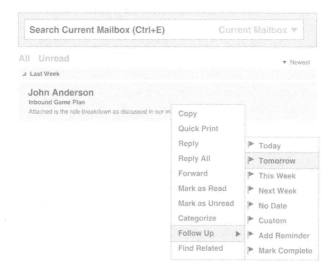

In the above screenshot I am saying, 'Follow Up' tomorrow. It now becomes a task on tomorrow's calendar. I then move the email to my Archive folder and it is now gone out of my Inbox and out of my way. The distraction is removed.

When tomorrow comes and I am looking at what I have to do for the day, I will see this email as a 'Follow Up' task with the attachment. At the time of the day when I am handling tasks, I will process this one carefully. Once I have processed the email, I can then mark it complete. The email is now gone from my 'Task' list.

The suggestion/tip is to learn how to use 'Tasks' and the 'Follow Up' flag as a way to handle emails by bringing the emails to a time and place when you are ready to deal with them. This gets them out of your Inbox and your headspace in the meantime.

Outlook Tip No. 3: Use 'Search'

Earlier in this chapter, we talked about using 'Search' to find emails instead of having multiple folders. The scenario we are dealing with now is that you have old emails in one 'Archive' folder or maybe in lots of different folders if you are not using this system. In either case, you now want to find an old email.

In your head you are thinking, 'I got an email from Slater? Was it to Anderson? Was it about updates?' What do you do?

Instead of crawling through multiple folders and looking for the needle in the haystack, put your cursor in the Outlook 'Search' box to access the Outlook 'Search' ribbon. Now you can use the ribbon to build your search or once you get used to 'Search', you can start typing, e.g. "*From:slater To:anderson update*". Search will hunt through all your email folders including the deleted and sent emails, and it will bring back any emails that satisfies these criteria.

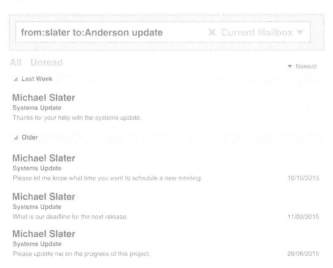

'Search' can be used to mimic your thought process and is

much faster than manually searching multiple folders. Learn how to use search. Take the five to ten minutes. It will save you a huge amount of time.

Outlook Tip No. 4: Use Tasks

We all have a "To-Do" list – or we should have! Why not manage your "To-Do" list in the Outlook 'Task' folder? Every time you think of something to do, just add a task to Outlook. There is also a nice feature called "recurring task". Every time you complete the task, it reappears one week or month later as you specify. Tasks can then be viewed:

- in the Outlook Task list
- in the Task pane of your Outlook calendar – so you can see the tasks for a particular day
- on your phone
- on a browser on any PC.

	OVERDUE	TODAY	TOMORROW	THIS WEEK	NO DATE
OVERDUE	Competitors Overview	Call with Blake	Send agenda	Check recurring billing	Two rivals surveys
	Board Meeting Charts	Attn: January		Sales Charts	Upward revisions
	Schedule a call with Mike	Add Glossary			
	Video Script Update				
NORMAL	Reporting Issues	Fwd. quarter report	Order login data	Login data	Design Meeting
	Germany sales report	App requirements	re: New items	New requirement	Re: blog post
	Corporate policy check		Reporting capabilities	Customer meeting	
	Email Issues				
LOW	Project Research	New proposal	Project Review	Final Review	Downtime estimate
	Emerging Trends	Check backup settings	Hardware invoice		New blog post
		Write job description			
		Content plan status			

Questions for an "email Management" REP

Start: Pick one of the Microsoft Outlook tips that you think might be of help and try it out when you are ready or feel the need to REP this area.

Evolve: Work the remaining tips that look useful in the weeks ahead as part of this REP.

Section 3. Situational Leadership

Introduction

The previous section explored elements of personal leadership. Managing your energy and time, developing a healthy attitude, and understanding your personality will make you happier and more effective personally and professionally. The next question is – how do you lead yourself in common situations with and for others?

> *"As a leader, you will never get ahead until your people are behind you."* – John C. Maxwell (1947-), Leadership Thinker

Motivation: Why does Situational Leadership Matter?

There are many common situations that you will find yourself in, such as meetings, making decisions, delivering presentations, working on teams and managing/leading teams (inside and outside of work). These situations involve you working with or for other people. This section of the handbook talks to how you might practice good leadership in the most common of these situations.

The Essence

In taking a proactive approach to situational leadership, you will be better placed to lead yourself and a team as the situation needs. It is important to develop a leadership style that works for you and also suits the context in which you find yourself. In these situations, you can and should give leadership, whether you are in charge or not.

Time Out

Think about your current leadership style. Do you have an approach or a set of approaches for the common situations you encounter?

What aspects would you like to work on and improve?

Manage Meetings (Ten Suggestions)

Introduction

"A meeting is an event where minutes are taken and hours wasted."

– James T. Kirk (William Shatner's character from Star Trek)

This quote is frequently cited about meetings but I cannot find the original source of the quote so it is likely not from the TV series Star Trek. However, it is a nice articulation of what many of us experience! Meetings are so often such a waste of time. Sad really.

Good meetings are essential to teamwork and collaborative management. Poor meetings are detrimental to group harmony and project success. Be intentional about how you participate in and facilitate meetings and do not take this for granted.

My test of a meeting is simple enough these days. Did we leave the meeting with more or less energy than we had beforehand? A good meeting should energize us. If you stop reading this chapter and get nothing more than the idea of this "meeting energy test", I feel your time will not have been wasted – unless of course you do not try out this test!

Motivation: Why Manage Meetings?

You need good meetings so the group you are working with feel connected, involved, and informed. You need positive meetings to make good decisions for people, teams and projects. Think of the cost of a poor meeting. Four people in a meeting for one hour is pretty close to one working day by the time you add up preparation time and follow-up. That is a lot of wasted time and energy, most especially if the meeting was not a positive experience for those involved. Poor meetings often lead to poor decisions, which carry the cost much further than the direct meeting time. Bad meetings can be very expensive in terms of time, money, motivation and energy.

The Essence

As you know by now, this handbook promotes the "Start|Evolve" approach to improvement. None of us have the time or the need to get every process perfect today. To paraphrase the 4th century North African bishop, Saint Augustine, *"Make me perfect, but not today Lord"*.

This chapter gives you one meeting practice to start with and nine further meeting practices to consider evolving with, and includes sample agendas for different types of meetings. This should give you a good start and from there you can evolve as needed.

Time Out

One of the main points of this chapter is that a meeting should leave the participants with the same, or ideally, more energy as they leave the meeting compared to when they walked in. Do your meetings achieve this? This is a simple but important situational leadership test.

Start with a Facilitator and Agenda

1. Have a DAFT meeting!

*"We will have **DAFT** meetings and by doing so we will be clear on: **D**esired outcome, **A**genda, **F**acilitator and **T**ake Aways."*

Be clear on what the **D**esired outcome of the meeting is and set the meeting **A**genda in service of the particular meeting objective. Ideally you should publish the desired outcome and agenda in advance of the meeting, so people know what to expect and can prepare (and to help remove any anxiety people might have).

Have a **F**acilitator, typically a Group or Project Manager, who starts the meeting by explaining the desired outcome of the meeting, proposes the agenda, and critically, keeps everyone to the agenda. A good facilitator will help attendees "park" items that are not essential to the desired outcome of this particular meeting. As you start a meeting, ask the team to be guided by the facilitator for this meeting.

I will say that not everyone has the skills of a good meeting facilitator. Either select a person with strong facilitation skills or have a person trained. As the leader, you may wish to ask someone else to facilitate the meeting for any one of three reasons. Firstly, you can focus more on the meeting content rather than the meeting process. Secondly, you may not be the best person to facilitate the meeting – this may not be your forte. Thirdly, you may wish to have people more involved and engaged on a team or project by being more collaborative.

As the meetings ends, be sure to summarize so people understand and agree the main Take Aways. Some people will have wandered mentally in the middle of the meeting, so this summary is an important way to make any decisions or actions items clear. If the meeting is important and you are worried that people may forget the key decisions and action items, ask one of the team to write-up the meeting minutes. So enjoy your **DAFT** meetings!

Evolve the Meeting Management Practices

You can evolve to meetings that are more successful by taking on board some of the extra nine practices below. Copy and adapt these practices as you see fit for use with your group.

2. Meeting Review

"We will review each meeting as it ends to see if it was a good meeting or not."

As the meeting ends, ask the participants, "How did we do on the energy test and with respect to meeting objectives?" If you get critical feedback, ask the team how to improve the next meeting. Of course, you need to be careful. You know the old joke about having two economists in the room and then having three opinions. With a collaborative team, you will have many opinions, and some may well be contradictory. That is the strength of a good team – many diverse inputs. Listen to the input of your team and decide what to accept. You cannot satisfy everyone. Select the ideas you feel will improve your meetings. Run your decisions by the team to get their understanding and agreement.

3. Small Meetings

"We will not invite people who do not really need to be there. Rather we will keep meetings as small as we can."

In many cases, I have found that small teams achieve more. Small teams tend to be effective and efficient. If you are inviting everyone just so they know what is going on, find other, more efficient ways to communicate. If you notice that people are inattentive or doing email while at your meeting, perhaps they do not need to be present. After the productive meeting with a smaller team you can communicate the outcome to the wider group.

4. Fewer Presentations

"We will not present at meetings. We will circulate the meeting materials three days in advance, so people can read in their own time and at their own pace."

The brain can read and process way faster than people can talk and present – maybe up to five times faster. I often see people daydream or do email when someone else is presenting at the meeting! Allied to this, we all process new information differently, so it is helpful to send the meeting materials in advance to let people prepare in their own way and in their own time. You can then spend the valuable meeting time talking about the materials rather than introducing them.

There are people who do not wish to send the materials in advance as they wish to control the presentation more. There are sensitive situations where this is indeed necessary, but not in most cases. I say circulate the materials in advance. Trust the team and then trust yourself to be able to facilitate a good meeting.

5. Prepare in Advance

"We will come prepared, or we will say we are not prepared."

I will cancel a meeting if I am not properly prepared in advance. I hate to waste everyone's time. If I am not prepared and it is vital to proceed with the meeting, then I will fess up so the meeting facilitator is aware and can adjust the meeting style as necessary.

6. Keep to Time

"We will start and finish on time. We will let the team know if we are running late and request their consent."

It is bad enough that meetings can be long, but when they run longer than scheduled, the rest of the day is delayed. If many people are at the meeting, these delays affect other people and groups not at the meeting. Sometimes this is necessary. However, more often than not, this is due to a poorly managed meeting. It can be very helpful to assign timings to an agenda to track as the meeting progresses. If you are running over on one item, maybe you defer an item to the next meeting so the meeting does not end late.

If you know that people are in back to back meetings, it is good to finish at least five minutes early, so that people have a break between meetings. You can also use the agenda to let the team know if the meeting is likely to run over in case anyone needs to leave.

7. Vary the Location and Style

"We will mix it up, e.g., walk outside while we meet, meet at a different location, invite an outside speaker / listener etc."

Funny how the world conspires to help us! As I was writing this section, a work colleague needed to talk through a difficult situation and get some inputs. Given that the day was sunny, we walked outside. This was a pleasant environment for a very difficult conversation. The situation in question was tight and tense, so it was good to get out of the office where there are less physical constraints.

If you have meetings that occur with great frequency and have the same agenda, people can get jaded. It is good to mix it up. Identify what works for you and your team. I must say that I do like to walk and talk. It suits my personal communication style.

It can also be good to get an outside speaker or listener. Recently, one of our projects had a quarterly review. For this review, we invited a retired leader to come and listen to our plans. He gave very good insights but also gave affirmation to the team, helping everyone know we were on the right path. The plans did not change that radically, but the team were more energized.

8. Active Listening

"We will properly listen before we comment."

There are times when we need to actively talk back and forth. There are also times we need to really listen, to actively listen, before we fully understand where someone is coming from. We have all experienced people who interrupt constantly, even if very politely ... "sorry for interrupting, but"! At meetings, I see some people physically shaking they are so anxious to speak and respond – but in some of these cases, I clearly have not yet made my main point! It is worth remembering that there is a reason that we were given two ears and one mouth! As a meeting facilitator, it is important to moderate so that the right balance of listening and talking takes place.

9. Pay Attention

"We will pay attention and we will not check email or phones."

I have been at meetings with people who miss the main points as they were checking email or phone messages and then delay everyone due to their inattentiveness. Someone who is talking or presenting may view this as disrespectful. Ask people not to check phones or emails, except in exceptional circumstances. Promise them a shorter, more effective meeting as a result.

10. Action Items

"We will take our action items seriously and complete them on time."

When the team complete their meeting action items on time, the project and the subsequent meetings proceed much smoother. As a team or project manager, you need to set this expectation. Thank people for timely completion of action items and call people out for the opposite – unless there are good reasons. Assuming you are running a DAFT meeting (as described above), then you will summarize the actions and main takeaway's as each meeting ends.

Other Ideas

I am in no way suggesting that the above meetings practices are the only or the best ones – but they are a good place to start. Pick and choose from the practices above as you see fit and then do some extra research to find other practices you would like to try.

Meeting Agenda Templates

The prior sections outlined a set of ten good meeting practices. I suggested that you start with one practice and if it works, evolve with more ideas from the list. The first practice on the list included the importance of having a meeting agenda. This section has sample templates for three common meeting types to help get you started. Enjoy!

Team Meetings

You do not want to have team meetings for the sake of meeting, so you do need to be careful with how these sessions are conducted. Here is a sample agenda you might consider using with your team.

1. Review and agree the meeting agenda with the team
2. Review, discuss and resolve any open issues
3. Look at upcoming work items for next week
4. Team process and approach – any adjustments needed?
5. (Time Permitting) Work achieved last week
6. AOB (Any Other Business)
7. Summarize the meeting outcomes.

These tips explain the suggested agenda further.

1. Review and agree meeting agenda with the team.
   - This brings the team to the same page as you start the meeting. Remember that the team are likely working on different tasks and sometimes on different projects (in a larger group), so this start of meeting alignment can be helpful and necessary.
2. Review, discuss and resolve any open issues.
   - I like to get the problems out of the way at the start of the meeting when energy levels are high.
   - As a leader, ask people for the issues and for their suggestions on how to address the issues. Do not assume in a collaborative group that you have to solve all issues by yourself. Set the opposite expectation with your team.
   - Be careful that the issues are "real issues".
   - When you start a meeting with the issue discussion, it shows you are realistic. By asking people to bring suggested resolutions to every issue, it shows you trust their judgement. It also shows that you expect people to take responsibility. This is very important and empowering for the team.
   - Sometimes the issue is so large that a separate meeting will be required (sometimes with different people) to resolve.
3. Look at upcoming work for next week.
   - What typically happens on teams is that work is defined in outline as a new project starts. As the timing of the work approaches, discussion and more definition is usually needed.

- There will be many tasks in the week ahead. You may not need to discuss them all. With the help of the team, select the key work items or deliverables on the dock for this week coming, and talk these through. Allow and encourage other team members to give inputs.
- This will help reduce surprises and eliminate any confusion around upcoming tasks.

4. Team process and approach – any adjustments needed?
   - There is no reason to assume that the decisions made in this early stage of this group setup are still 100% correct. Maybe it is time to adjust some aspect of how the team is coordinated or managed. Now is a good time to check.
   - This is a respectful reflection to offer team members on a collaborative endeavor. It explains that team members have a real say in how the group is run.

5. (Time Permitting) Work achieved last week.
   - If time permits, it is good to review the work or at least the highlight tasks from last week.
   - You might be wondering why this is so late in the agenda. I find that people will talk at length about what was achieved at the expense of talking about what is yet to be achieved. Do not let the meeting descend into a history lesson as the meeting starts! It will steal too much valuable group meeting time.
   - If you would like to highlight work completed, send a quick update email to the team after the meeting.

6. AOB (Any Other Business).
   - At this stage of the meeting, cover any small points or items that need attention but this should not take up the entire meeting. Keep the front part of the meeting free for the more important items.

7. Summarize the meeting outcomes.
   - Recap the meeting in terms of decisions, outcomes, or action items, or all of the above.
   - If required, circulate meeting minutes with detail of items covered, decisions made, assigned tasks and any agenda items not covered.

Problem Solving / Creative Meetings

Problems and challenges occur in most group work. Creative solutions are always needed to deliver on some of the requirements. The team generally has or can come up with the solutions. You just need to give people the time and space. There are many ways to run a brainstorm / problem solving style of meeting. The "ABCD" agenda works well in these situations.

1. **A**gree the **A**im of the meeting and **A**sk lots of questions.
2. **B**rainstorm in a **B**lue sky (open, creative, and imaginative, with no limits or boundaries) manner all the possibilities. Allow no critique at this stage and instead encourage questions to clarify.
3. Enter into a robust but respectful set of **C**onversations with healthy **C**ritique and lots of **C**onstructive **C**onflict. At this point in the agenda, it is important to push the boundaries of the ideas being proposed.
4. **D**iscuss lots and with as much consensus and inputs as possible, make good **D**ecisions. Include a mechanism to check the outcome.

Once your team becomes familiar with this template, you can use a shorter version of the "ABCD" agenda.

Shorter Option:
1. **A**sk questions; **A**gree the **A**im
2. **B**lue-sky **B**rainstorm
3. **C**ritique with **C**onflict
4. **D**iscuss and **D**ecide.

Shortest Option:
1. **A**im
2. **B**rainstorm
3. **C**ritique
4. **D**ecide.

Project Sponsor Meetings

If you are on a tough project, it is important to have a Project Sponsor in your corner. Indeed most projects will benefit from and need a Project Sponsor. More on this topic in 'Section 4 – Collaborative Project Management'. Very good sponsors are really busy, so you need to make good use of the meeting to gain their respect and thus their help. Here is a sample agenda that you might consider using with your Project Sponsor:

1. Review and agree the meeting agenda
2. Update on progress to goals
3. Resolve open risks, issues or change requests
4. Review pending decisions
5. Other feedback for the project manager?
6. Any Other Business (AOB)
7. Summarize the meeting outcomes.

Here are some tips to make the most of this agenda outline.

1. Review and agree the meeting agenda.
   - Agree the desired meeting outcome. Explain to the sponsor what it is you wish to achieve and ask what they want to get from the meeting.
   - The sponsor might not be thinking about your project as you meet, so this is a good way to get alignment as you start the meeting.
2. Update on progress to agreed goals.
   - The sponsor will want to know where you are with the project, even if only at a high level, before they relax into helping you with the project success
   - Ideally, use pre-agreed dashboards with the schedule, KPIs, status reports, etc. when giving this update. This will give the sponsor confidence in your management ability and saves meeting time. It will also allow the project sponsor to self-report, and stay connected and involved between meetings.
   - In an ideal world the sponsor will have read materials before the meeting, but it is wise not to assume this is the case with busy people.
3. Resolve open risks, issues or change requests.
   - As part of this sponsor meeting, you should acknowledge, understand, and deal with any big rocks in the way of project success. Typically, these are risks, issues or change requests. These rocks may also change the project outcomes, so the sponsor needs to know and have the chance to input.
   - A later chapter of the handbook (in Section 4 – Collaborative Project Management) will explain

"Stage 4 – Track and Re-Plan the Project". This later chapter outlines a set of steps to help bring the project back in line with the project goals.

4. Review pending decisions.
   - A stitch in time saves nine. It can help to talk the project sponsor through any major decisions you are about to make and get inputs to save time later on.

5. Other feedback for the project manager?
   - It is always good to ask the sponsor for other inputs or feedback.
   - You will typically get some extra advice from a good project sponsor. And it shows you are open to feedback, which is also important.

6. AOB (Any Other Business).
   - At this stage of the meeting, cover any small points or items that need attention but should not take up the entire meeting. Keep the front part of the meeting free for the more important and difficult items.

7. Summarize the meeting outcomes.
   - Recap the meeting in terms of decisions, outcomes, or action items, or all of the above.
   - If required, circulate meeting minutes with the detail of items covered, decision made, assigned tasks and any agenda items not covered.

Summary of Manage Meetings

Start with one or two of these practices explained above, and with these first practices, experience and enjoy success. Once the initial success has been experienced, select and adopt some of the other practices.

- We will have **DAFT** meetings and we will be clear on: **D**esired outcome, **A**genda, **F**acilitator and **T**ake Aways.
- Meeting Review: We will review each meeting as it ends to see if it was a good meeting or not.
- Small Meetings: We will not invite people who do not really need to be there. Rather we will keep meetings small.
- Fewer Presentations: We will not present at meetings. We will circulate the meeting materials three days in advance, so people

can read in their own time and at their own pace.

- Prepare in Advance: We will come prepared, or we will say we are not prepared.
- Keep to Time: We will start and finish on time. We will let the team know if we are running late and request their consent.
- Vary the Location and Style: We will mix it up, e.g., walk outside while we meet, meet at a different location, invite an outside speaker / listener, etc.
- Active Listening: We will properly listen before we comment
- Pay Attention: We will pay attention and we will not check email or phones.
- Action Items: We will take our action items seriously and complete them on time.

It is not at all hard to run good meetings, but you need to be intentional and make it a priority. I wish you good energy meetings!

Questions for a "Meetings" REP

Does your team need better meetings?

Start: Select one or two of the above practices to get your project meeting management to where it needs to be when you are ready or feel the need to REP this area.

Evolve: Cycle through these practices and over the course of a few weeks and months make more improvements that are relevant to your meeting management.

Deliver Impactful Presentations (Eight Steps)

Introduction

"Words are, of course, the most powerful drug used by mankind."
– Rudyard Kipling, Speech to the Royal College of Surgeons in London, 1923.

I see so many good people with great ideas that are not heard. It is not that the people in question do not try to explain the ideas; it is just that the communication is unintentionally poor. Often times my mind will wander as I wonder if this person will ever get to the point! The ideas, message, suggestions, requests can easily get lost in a sea of excess words or a haze of obscurity.

Motivation: Why Put Energy into Presentations?

It can frequently take a long time to figure a problem, to craft a strategy. This journey, the time spent at this investigative stage helps us get intimately acquainted with the issues at hand. Why not put extra time into preparing to communicate the essence of the message to those who were not part of the same journey. Be sure that the hard work and creativity get a fair hearing.

The Essence

You have ideas and a great presentation can turn these ideas into reality. This chapter suggests eight tips to deliver great presentations to get your message across, to get a fair hearing.

Time Out

Have you been at a meeting or presentation recently that bored or confused you? What might have the presenter done different to reverse that situation? Have you delivered a presentation or a key message at a meeting (formally or informally) that did not go as you had hoped? What might you have done different to reverse this outcome?

Decide the Message

Decide the one laser message that you wish to deliver. Think through the key and compelling take away that you wish your audience to be thinking and believing as you finish. If you are not clear on the message, then how can you expect your audience to be aligned?

Start Strong

Start Strong and really grab the attention of the group in front of you or around the table with you. Do not start in the traditional manner of introducing yourself, your group, etc. This is boring! It is safe to assume that the minds of the majority of the group are not on your topic as you start and you should assume that you need to get them tuned in to you. When you start strong, the audience will be more relaxed and will start to believe that you are not going to waste their valuable time.

How do you do this? Maybe you paint a picture of what the future would, could or should look like. Perhaps you start with an outrageous statement. It is often good to start with a searching question. Maybe you can summarize the problem at hand (making it obvious) and move to a compelling solution. You want to start strong that you can visibly see a difference in the attention rates of the audience.

Structure with a Few Key Points

In the body of your presentation, share a few (not too many – three often works well) key concepts that you wish to convey. You may well have ten key points you would like to make, but consider this: will people remember ten points? Will they get bored or lost mid-way through and forget what you are really trying to achieve. Do you really need to convey ten points to get your main message across?

In terms of structuring the body of your presentation, you might have had a debate teacher in school who gave the following good advice: *"as you start tell them what you are going to say, then tell them what you want to convey, and then as you finish remind them what you just told them!"* . It is good for your presentation to have a start, middle and end.

We all get distracted very easily in presentations. There are so many thoughts, ideas, feelings, and incoming messages competing for our attention. You would want to be an amazing presenter to completely hold our attention for half an hour or more. With this in mind, as you present, do not be afraid to repeat some of the same words/phrases that you want people to be saying after your presentation. Repetition works!

Explain using Stories

We like to listen to stories. We relate to and learn more easily from stories. Details, we get lost in. If you tell a good story, people will remember your presentation. Use a story where possible in your presentation to explain the concept, idea or issue at hand.

Speak Authentically for Your Audience

It is clear that you want something to happen as a result of this presentation, but be careful not to make it be all about you. Consider that you are talking to this group for a reason – and likely it is that you need their support with next steps. Put yourself in their shoes. In advance, think through what are their needs, wants, desires? Then speak for and not to the audience. Present as if you and the audience were one and the same. Somehow, create an emotional connection. Have a heartfelt conversation with the audience. Whatever you do, do not lecture them. If you speak for and with the audience and not to the audience, then you have a much better chance of having the presentation come across as a presentation, rather than lecture. And, who wants to be lectured to? It is important to be yourself, not a phoney. Above all, be passionate and authentic. If you come across as not caring about the topic, why should they care?

Vary the Delivery

Given our short attention spans, it is wise to vary your tone, speed and pitch as you present. It is good to pause every now and again, to give people time to think. Do not be afraid to use visual gestures. Include visuals on your slides and short video clips where it makes sense. Be very careful not to have too many words on your slides, as it greatly distracts from your presentation, as some people will attempt to read and will tune out from your delivery. How you deliver the message is as important as the message. Prepare to do both well.

Close Strong

You are about to close the presentation. This is your last chance (for now) to get your message across. Bear in mind that many people may have lost you mid-way through, but you now have one last chance to get their attention and support. More often than not, people want to believe they can reach the concept/message/state that you are presenting on. You now have a final opportunity to make them believe that they can. It is also a good idea, as you close, to link back to the opening. Above all, as you close, let your conviction come through again.

Prepare, Rehearse, Revise

Practice makes perfect. There are no short cuts. The above tips work really well, but they require thought and time. You need to put in the time to think through and map out your presentation. Then you need to take the time to rehearse the presentation aloud, as if for real, and perhaps with a sample audience. This will give you great feedback and you will then want to revise aspects of your presentation.

Fear of Public Speaking

Many people have a fear of public speaking. I find this very natural. After all people have a fear of driving, until they learn how to drive and have real driving experience. If you are one of these people, preparing in advance will be of immense help, as you will know what you are going to say. This will boost your confidence. However, it will not be enough! You also need to practice aloud, multiple times. This will give you more confidence. You may still be nervous before you speak, and that is natural enough, but you will be much more confident in your message and your ability to deliver it. To overcome most of the fears of public speaking, remember to keep cycling through – Prepare, Rehearse, Revise.

Summary of Deliver Impactful Presentations

Some presentations are very significant and can be to a large group. Other presentations are less important and for a small group. However, they are all presentations. You are trying to get your message across. Be intentional about this.

Some or all of the following tips will be very helpful as you present your ideas to groups of people you want to bring on board with you:

- Decide the key message that you wish to impart before you present.
- Start your presentation strong, in way that really grabs the attention of the audience.
- Structure your presentation with a beginning, a middle and an end.
- Tell stories that get your message across. A picture or a story paints a thousand words.
- Do not lecture your audience; be authentic; speak for and not to them.
- Vary your voice (tone, pitch, speed) and use different media (images, pictures, videos).
- Close your presentation very strong. This is your last chance!
- Prepare your presentation. Rehearse your presentation. Revise your presentation. Repeat in a loop until ready.

Questions for a "Presentation" REP

How do you rate your ability to deliver presentations that have an impact?

Start: Try one or two of the above ideas the next time you present and afterwards reflect on how the presentation went.

Evolve: Come back later when you are ready or feel the need to REP this area and try more of the tips, eventually building up to one presentation where you try all or most of the tips on one presentation. Share these eight steps with a colleague and ask your friend to give you feedback on your presentation.

Make Good Decisions (Individual and Team)

Introduction

> *"Most high officials leave office with the perceptions and*
> *insights with which they entered; they learn how to make decisions*
> *but not what decisions to make."*
> – Henry A. Kissinger (Secretary of State, US, Sept. 1973 to Jan. 1977)

I believe that Henry Kissinger has it right. We really learn to make decisions once we start management. When I think back on my own training, decision-making was not a topic we studied very formally. However, on reflection, making good decisions is a key part of living, management and leadership, and making transparent decisions with teams is a critical part of Personal and Collaborative Leadership. This chapter will guide you through some simple models to make good decisions (both alone and with a group) and will briefly discuss the role of personality in decision-making.

Motivation: Why Focus on Decision Making?

Personal Decisions: Many decisions you make affect your mood, your disposition, and ultimately, your leadership (inside and outside of work). It is important for you to make good decisions for you. If you are happy as a person, then this will come across to the team and will help the team morale. It is also important for your team that you make and facilitate good decisions.

Work Decisions: Every decision you make at work helps or hinders the team. Each decision can make the work shorter or longer, less or more expensive, simpler or more complex. Each decision can improve or dis-improve team morale, making the group feel better or worse about their participation on the team.

The Essence

Have a considered approach to make decisions. Some decisions are for you to make alone and some need to be made with others. It is desirable to involve others collaboratively in key team or group decisions. For significant decisions, communicate the intended decision making process upfront and later share the results.

Time Out

How do you make decisions today? Reflect on some of the decisions you made recently at work or in your personal life. Think through some of the larger life decisions you have made over the years.

Making Decisions – Using Your Gut

Most of our decisions are made on gut instinct in a matter of seconds and usually less than a minute. This is the most common way to make a decision. Sometimes you just know the right decision and the right course of action is obvious. If you know, you know! And if you are right, then you have nothing to worry about.

However, what if you are wrong? If you are wrong, you will find out or be found out. If you make an instant decision, be prepared to adjust if you are wrong. Be courageous, flexible, and open enough to reverse the decision if it is wrong. Not everybody finds this easy, but it represents the best of honest leadership.

Making Decisions – a Holistic Approach

One version of a holistic decision-making process is as follows:
- Remember the privilege of choice
- Frame the decision
- Start with indifference
- Continue with a head/logical decision
- Confirm with a heart decision.

A tip from my grandfather: do not make an important decision when you are feeling bad. You may well make a very poor decision. Wait until you feel better.

Remember the Privilege of Choice

We can sometimes feel burdened by pending decisions and this is understandable. However, many times the decisions represent choices between options that all improve the situation. In these cases, it is important to cut ourselves some slack and enjoy the decision making process. Remember that in many situations, we are electing which path to follow – it is our choice. In decision making, try to enjoy the freedom of choice and free will that we have.

Frame the Decision

Name and frame the reason for the decision. Remember, some items are not really up for decision, so be careful not to bring every matter through a decision making process. For example, you are behind on the project and you would like to bring on two more people to the project, but your sponsor has explicitly said that the resources at this stage of the project are fixed. Save yourself and others the energy and stress. At this stage, decide if there really is a decision to be made. Then frame the decision to be made.

Start with Indifference

Sometimes the decision is not obvious; you need time and a decision-making process. If you need time to make the right decision, do not start with the decision already made in your head. Do not have the end (a pre-ordained decision) justified by the means (a biased decision-making process). Start by being indifferent, unbiased, and impartial. Move yourself to this more neutral state. Desire the right outcome. If this is a work related decision, remind yourself of the group objectives or goals. If this is a personal decision, be mindful of your own goals and values. This level of detachment can be quite difficult but it is important and will help you to make a much better decision.

Continue with a Head / Logical Decision

You can now continue the decision-making process with a logical approach. Some suggested steps follow:

- Question: Start by listing the questions that are on your mind and start to answer the questions as best you can at this stage.
- Research: Do some desk research:
    - Gather more data/information
    - Research so you are not limited by what you know.
- Consult: Ask for help with the decision. Consult with those involved and LISTEN
    - Get other perspectives but be mindful that you may still be making the decision yourself.

- <u>Analyse</u>: List the options that you now believe you have. Lay out and weigh up the pros and cons of each option. List the advantages or benefits of each choice. Also, list the disadvantages or potential damages of each option.
- <u>Decide</u>: Make a reasoned decision:
  - After the research, consultation and analysis, if you are sure that the decision is right and obvious, then run with it. Commit to the decision and get fully behind it. Give it every chance of success. Commit.
  - If this is a big decision, do not confirm the decision immediately, but pause and confirm with a heart decision (see description below).
- <u>Communicate</u>: Talk through the decision and the rationale with those involved.
- <u>Act</u>: Take the actions that the decision warrants.
- <u>Reflect</u>: If this is a big decision, set aside future time to reflect on the actual outcome versus the desired outcome.

Confirm with a Heart Decision

It can happen that you have to make a big decision but you have the luxury of a few extra days. Moreover, for important decisions, you should take the extra time.

After you make the reasoned decision following a process like the one above, you can sit with the decision and see if you still feel mostly positive about the decision after a few hours and a few days - not just immediately. Over these days, assume the decision is made and imagine what it is like to live with that decision. Listen to what your heart is telling you. Follow your feelings (the good and the bad) and try to understand them. Do not go final on the decision when you feel bad about it. Let it settle.

If the decision is a significant life decision and you are still somewhat unsure, then ask yourself the deathbed question. Imagine you are at the point of death and you are reviewing your life. Do you think you would be happy with this decision or not? This may seem a bit dramatic, but in certain situations, it will help.

You can also use the "other person" technique to check difficult decisions. Imagine you are advising someone making this same decision (someone you love, respect and want the best for). What advice would you give this person who was at this stage of the decision-making process? How would you advise this person to proceed on the right course of action? This can help to guide you.

I was surprised with an invitation to join the international board of an amazing not-for-profit. Even though I felt extremely honoured by the invitation, my gut told me it would not make sense to take on this additional responsibility. I already had too much on my plate. Moreover, I was not sure I had the relevant experience to help this organization. Yet, something did not seem right about saying No, so I ran the decision through the full logical decision making process described here, and the decision still came out as a No. I sat with the decision for a few days and in the end, I was not able to say No. In this case, I followed my heart and said Yes. I have to say that I am now really happy with this decision!

Making Decisions – with a Group

There are many ways to make decisions with a group.

- **Autocratic**: You are the leader and you make the decision. There are times (e.g. dire emergencies or routine decisions) when you will not have time or a need to consult with a wider group, and this approach is appropriate. However, this approach to making decisions is not very empowering. Will people be inclined to make good decisions when you are not around? Surely, you do not wish to control every decision. This style of decision making for all decisions could eventually cripple you and the team.

- **Consensus**: You bring everyone together and keep them together until consensus is reached. And, there are times when you may feel you need to get absolutely everyone on board with a decision. However, even though you feel this need, it is not always possible for so many reasons. And, I sometimes wonder do we exaggerate the need our people have to be involved in every decision. Apart from the fact that this approach is expensive, this approach to making a decision can be very tiring and really sap the energy of the people involved.

- **Majority Rule**: You vote at the end of a meeting (after lots of positive open discussions) on the best course of action. This is my least favorite, as you might be overlooking some expertise/facts or deep feelings that go against the majority opinion. To paraphrase many wiser than me, democracy is not the best form of government, just appears to be the safest.

- **Consultative**: In this approach, you give someone the power to make the decision and make him or her accountable for the outcome of the decision. However, you set the expectation that this person must consult with a subset of people who will be affected by the decision and also consult with colleagues who have real expertise in this arena. In this consultative process, everyone knows who is empowered and entrusted to make the decision. In addition, the responsibility for different decisions rotates to different people, which means many people are involved in this process in different roles, and they come to respect the process more as times goes on. This also has the advantage of reducing politics and in-company lobbying from decision-making. I really like this approach to decision making.

Tapping into Group Creativity

In workshops on team collaboration, I ask this question, "What helps group creativity and decision making?" I tend to get answers like chaos, critique, constructive conflict, and other varied inputs. When I ask the same group the following question, "What hinders group creativity and decision making?", I get a very similar list!

You want and need to involve the team in making creative and solid decisions but you need an approach, a process. In an earlier chapter, "Manage Meetings (Ten Suggestions)", we explained the "ABCD" agenda for creative problem solving. This can work very well to involve the group in making tough decisions. You can find more detail on this topic in that earlier chapter, but here is a summary of an agenda for such a group session:

1. **A**gree the **A**im (e.g. what do we aim to decide)
2. **B**rainstorm in a **B**lue sky manner
3. **C**ritique with lots of **C**onstructive **C**onflict
4. **D**iscuss and make good **D**ecisions.

Making Decisions – and Project Management

Decision points occur at all five stages of Collaborative Project Management. Spoiler alert! In the next 'Section 4 – Collaborative Project Management,' we will introduce a simple but effective five-stage model, depicted here. As a project manager, you need to merge decision-making approaches (as covered in this chapter) with your knowledge and experience of project management practices and the specific context of your team and project.

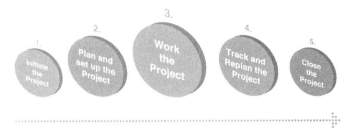

Making Decisions – and Personality Types

Time Out

Think about how personality can affect decision-making. How does your personality affect your decision-making?

Some people are, by their very nature, indecisive. They find it quite difficult to make most decisions. I often find these people very loyal to the decision when they do make it. I am sure you know people like this. Other people make decisions way too quickly without considering all the consequences. These people are more impulsive. Our personality preferences certainly influence our decision making style.

How you primarily react to the world will affect your decision making process. There are many ways to describe how we react to the world, but one simple way is to say that we react from the head, heart or gut.

Head centred	More logical in our reasoning	I think, therefore I am
Heart centred	More emotional about life	I feel, therefore I am
Gut centred	Just know and do not think or feel as much	I know, therefore I am

Is one of the above more naturally prevalent in how you react to the world? If so, be aware of this when making decisions. A good decision is made when the three centres (i.e. head, heart and gut) are eventually in balance, as described in the holistic decision making approach above.

The Credits

Credit where credit is due. Much of the content in this chapter is adapted from a subset of the decision making practices as explained by Ignatius of Loyola in his landmark book, 'The Spiritual Exercises', from 1548. In these Exercises, Ignatius calls these ways to make 'elections'. Amazing to think that I reach back to 1548 for decision-making practices. However, at another level it is not so amazing, as making decisions is a fundamental part of being human and the human condition was not invented this century!

Summary of Make Good Decisions

Hard decisions are just hard. There is no getting away from this. However, we can make them somewhat easier by having an approach. If the decision is easy, a gut decision will typically be right. If the decision is hard, then it will be fruitful to follow a holistic decision-making process starting with a head decision and confirming with a heart perspective. There are also different approaches to making a decision with a group and I recommend you try the Consultative approach as it is described above to see how it works for you.

Questions for a "Decisions" REP

Where do you now stand on your decision-making approaches and practices?

Start: Set a goal to practice some of the types of decision making in your professional or personal life when you are ready or feel the need to REP this area.

Evolve: Reflect on and summarise the decision-making processes that works best for you. Decide if you need to do more research and work on your decision-making.

Give Everyone a Voice (Strategy and Tactics)

"Find your voice and inspire others to find theirs."

– *Stephen R. Covey, The 8th Habit: From Effectiveness to Greatness*

Introduction

I try to be in Galway for two weeks in the middle of July each year for the Galway International Arts Festival. It is an amazing array of theatre, circus, music, dance, visual arts, comedy and insightful talks. In July 2017, I cycled in to Eyre Square on a beautiful Saturday afternoon to see the citizens of Galway help build a reconstruction of the Aula Maxima (which means, Great Hall) from cardboard boxes. The Aula is the original and beautiful centrepiece of the university in Galway city, built in 1845. The 2017 Arts Festival version was a spectacular re-construction.

What made this construction project so special was that the people of and visitors to Galway city built it together on that day. There was no crew pre-selection, no training, and no months of pre-build. People, young and old, mostly children, just showed up and built this structure from cardboard boxes over the course of that day! All the people I met and observed were freely giving of their time to this build project and loved it. And, the next afternoon, the people came back and happily de-constructed the model Aula to return Eyre Square (in Galway city centre) to it's original form.

Motivation

Wouldn't you love to lead or be part of a fabulous team that delivered on something special, and had fun in the process? Of course, you would! The Arts often depicts what happens in life. In this case, it would be wonderful if we could get life to imitate the Arts!

The Essence

As I made the cycle home on that sunny afternoon, I noodled what had just happened. I wondered how 'The People Build' team delivered on this. They got blank strangers to come together to build something wonderful in a few hours. I was very taken with this leadership achievement. I started to think through the likely elements of their strategy. I ran repeatedly through many possible elements and kept re-ordering them, again and again. It was a fascinating mind puzzle. Thinking back on it, it is a surprise that I did not crash the bike, or end up at a different place to home, I was that consumed by figuring what I had just witnessed! By the time I reached home, I had settled on these five ingredients in this order: Vision, Organization, Ingenuity, Collaboration and Engagement. I scribbled them down on a piece of paper and it is only today, one year later, as the 2018 Galway International Arts Festival is almost upon on us, that I am writing them up! Better late, than never! This year in the 2018 Arts festival, the people will build a giant floating bridge, again made from thousands of cardboard boxes.

The leaders of this project did really give everyone a VOICE. This, to me, was the magic, the essence of the strategy. The main aim of this chapter is to examine this leadership strategy. The chapter talks to the idea that everyone should have a voice and at the same time walks through five elements of leadership.

If to 'Give Everyone a VOICE' is a strategy for a team, group or project, there are many examples of simple tactics that adopt that approach. Two such approaches are covered later in this chapter. Both detail tactics to give everyone a voice by eliciting feedback in a structured, comprehensive and at the same time, positive and engaging manner.

Time Out

Can you remember a project or a team where you genuinely believed that your voice and that of everyone else was really heard and deeply listened to? What did that feel like? What was the outcome of this endeavour? Is this part of your leadership style?

The VOICE Strategy

It would be possible to give everyone a voice and have everything descend into chaos. People might wisecrack that this is what happens with some democratically elected governments! Intuitively we know that to give everyone a voice is a strategy that can and should work, if we trust and execute well.

V – Vision

I suspect that someone or group set or facilitated a vision in the Galway Arts Festival. In this case, I assume the vision was to build a replica of the Aula Maxima in Galway City using cardboard boxes and to involve as many people as possible in the construction. The vision articulated was perhaps as simple as an "Aula Maxima rebuild, by the people for the people". That vision would have been very clear and easy to visualize and at the same time novel, fun and compelling.

In team or situational leadership, it is very important to have a vision and to be able to articulate this vision in a way that captures the imagination of people. It is also important to allow people feedback and shape the vision that the group are going to take on.

Sometimes leaders find it hard to articulate a vision, but they have a clear purpose. They are not sure exactly what they want to do; they have no clear vision yet. However, they have a purpose, a why. They know that something must be done, for some reason that is obvious to them. In time, they figure the what, the vision. Purpose can also be very compelling. Some would argue that purpose is more compelling than vision. Either way, a vision or purpose that people can understand, question, critique, and buy into is a wonderful place to start or re-start an endeavour.

For your project, team, group or organization, do you have a clear vision or purpose that people have the chance to understand, shape, and be excited by?

O – Organization

I saw individuals and teams of people guided by facilitators build the Aula model. The facilitators helped the volunteer builders understand the organization, and they had the opportunity to join different teams. The novice builders were either assembling the cardboard boxes or adding the boxes to different parts of the new structure. Everyone had a role to play, a job to do, and box by box, the replica of the Aula was built. The organization was relaxed, enjoyable and informal but very clear.

Let me digress for a moment to a different but also a wonderful story: the Galway team playing in the national Hurley final in Ireland in September 2017, hoping for victory for the first time in almost thirty years. Hurley, an Irish invention, is the fastest field game in the world and a very high-octane sport. I was lucky enough to be at this All Ireland final and thankfully, Galway did win. It was a sublime team performance. The teamwork on display was mesmeric. One of the Galway players was asked what it was like playing in this noisy cauldron, and how did the players hear each other's instructions. The player responded that there was not much need for talking, as the game was naturally so fast, and everyone knew what he had to do. There was a game plan and also a plan if the game plan did not work. All was clear. Each player had a clear role and set of responsibilities. Magical!

For your project, team, group or organization, do you have a clear organization, where everyone knows who needs to do what? Moreover, have your team had a voice in understanding and shaping this organization and way of working?

I – Ingenuity

Back to the Aula model build example; creating a large model from cardboard boxes is very clever. 'Employing' a volunteer workforce to build this model is a great strategy. Making this be part of an Arts Festival when people are looking for fun and entertainment shows an impeccable sense of timing. The whole project is backed by a great idea. The approach to success in this case is ingenious.

Great projects to be successful need a spark. They require some ingenuity. They benefit greatly from some smart recipe for success.

What is the spark of ingenuity, the difference that your project, team, group or organization leans on? Have your team had the chance to understand, shape, and be excited by this spark of genius?

C – Collaboration

The Aula model build in this Arts festival had people who had never met before collaborating in minutes. It was very impressive. Moreover, how could a large-scale model of the Aula be constructed in one day, if people were not collaborating. It would not be possible. Collaboration is an essential ingredient of team success. In addition, these strangers really enjoyed working together. They had fun.

Just think through the opposite. You are on a project where people do not willingly collaborate. No fun! Life is too short for this type of work environment.

For your project, team, group or organization, have you a willing and strong spirit of collaboration? If the answer is 'yes', then enjoy the journey with your team. You have something special. If the answer is otherwise, then give your team a voice in helping you shape the collaboration needed. People are very smart. Consult the team and ask, listen carefully and then be willing to adjust.

E – Engagement

The 'workers' on this Aula model build were very engaged. They were really into it. They seemed totally committed to me, for the while they were there. They were giving it everything. This high level of engagement was necessary to have this model completed in one day.

You do not have to search too hard on the internet for surveys reporting the typically low levels of employee engagement in organizations. It is frightening. Work is such a massive part of life and we deserve to be engaged. To me, it is a human right.

For your project, team, group or organization, have you a high and healthy level of engagement? If the answer is 'no', do you know why? Maybe you should ask your team and give them a voice in helping you deliver the level of engagement needed. Your team will have good answers, if you trust them, and if you are prepared to be humble enough to deeply listen.

KARA – A Friendly Feedback Tactic

The last few pages describe an overarching strategy where real leadership gives everyone a voice, and it calls out five key areas in particular. I hope this gives you some ideas for your own leadership in whatever situation you find yourself. This next section describes the first of two simple but effective feedback tactics to hear these voices and very importantly to have each voice hear the other voices.

We often ask others for feedback or they ask us for our

feedback, and in these situations, it is important to make the most of the opportunity. In feedback situations, it is important to be able to give feedback so it is balanced and so that people really hear it. Likewise, it is key that you really hear the feedback to your ideas. I have seen it happen so many times that the manner in which the feedback is delivered or received negates the real value hiding in the feedback. Ironically, the more people shout, the less we can hear them!

The word "cara" in the Irish language means friend. Very often people see feedback as hostile and yet feedback should be helpful and honest – just like a true friend. For the purposes of this technique we will mis-spell "cara" as "kara", as it will make our mnemonic easier to remember! Here follows the very simple KARA protocol to ask people to use when giving written or verbal feedback.

To start the feedback process, someone needs to explain the idea or thoughts, maybe verbally or perhaps with a document. It is good at this stage to answer questions to help clarify and further explain the ideas. This ensures that people have a common understanding of what it is they are giving feedback on. Then you ask people to provide their KARA feedback:

- Keep
- Adjust
- Remove
- Add

Keep: It is always good to have people start with the positive aspect of the feedback. It helps the person giving the feedback as much as the person receiving the feedback. Some people are naturally very critical, and while this is a key skill and an important role for a team, it is often a poor way to start giving feedback. In addition, you will often find that these people focus so much on what needs to be fixed, that they often miss what is good. In some situations, they do not miss what is good, rather they neglect to cite the good. In this case the person receiving the feedback, may not know that there is good perceived. Ask people to start the feedback with what is good and worth preserving from the ideas. Moreover, if you are giving feedback, you can lead by example, and start by commenting on the good worth keeping.

Adjust: Move next to what needs to be changed and needs adjusting. Some of the initial ideas might be on the right track, but in need of some tweaking, some re-alignment. This is also positive and helpful feedback. Be honest.

Remove: Many ideas or proposals contain extra ideas that are not necessary, or not needed at the current stage. It is best to hear this feedback sooner. It is helpful to get feedback on what needs to be removed, deleted at the earliest stage possible. Be very clear.

Add: A creative process will always add new ideas to the mix. Once a person or a group get into a flow, there will typically be a flow of creativity, which is productive and also fun. It is so much more positive to say that you have ideas to add to the mix, than to say that the person forgot many items! In this simple KARA protocol, you are striving to facilitate a flow of helpful feedback that is not tainted by negativity. Be very open.

Working in a group, people are not always good at listening. Moreover, you find that people are at different points in their thought process. Some people want to explain what is missing, while others are in the adjust zone. Sadly, some people can be in bad form and just want to moan! By using this simple KARA protocol, you can have the group move and communicate in unison. This protocol also encourages the kind of positive but honest interactions that you believe are helpful.

You need to remember that not everyone is open to feedback on his or her ideas. I bet you have met people who are closed! Moreover, it is good to remember your intention. Hopefully, your intention is positive and not destructive. Ideally, you want to give constructive and helpful feedback, as any good team player would. You also want to encourage others to give positive and helpful feedback and this simple KARA pattern is designed to facilitate same.

Team Examen

In the 'Manage Your Energy' chapter in section 2 a gratitude and reflection Examen was introduced as a positive emotional energy practice. The Examen can also be used in a team setting to give everyone a voice and to still people for long enough so they can hear their own voice. You might walk a team through an Examen to help re-align the team, to assist the team to get back on track and critically to foster open and honest communications. Here are three simple steps you can ask each person to sit quietly and reflect on once a week and afterwards to share openly:

- What are you grateful for about this team or how we have progressed in the past week? As that which you are grateful for comes to mind, savor the good feeling of this positive team dynamic or outcome.
- Secondly, reflect on how the team has proceeded in the past week, the good and the bad, by rummaging through the team activities, day by day, or activity by activity. As you remember each item, you might move on quickly or you might reflect on some more carefully. Maybe you are happy with how we as a team managed each situation and maybe not. Perhaps with the benefit of hindsight, we could have handled some of the situations better.
- Thirdly, decide how you want next week to proceed on our team, mindful of what you are grateful for and what you learned from looking back on the last week.

This 'Team Examen' can of course be facilitated daily, weekly, monthly, quarterly or coincident with a significant team milestone. The key is to give people on the team time and space to stop and think. Thereafter, you do want the members of the team to share what they thought, felt and learned during this important reflection.

Summary

A good leader will assist people to find their voice and then give everyone a voice as a natural part of working with a team. A good leader will always listen. And people will feel that they have been heard. By contrast, a poor leader will monopolize the conversations and will seek to have their voice be the dominant one. People on the team will find this very frustrating and annoying.

There are so many situations where we as leaders need to listen and these five areas are key topics to listen to people and give them an active voice on: Vision, Organization, Ingenuity, Collaboration and Engagement.

Strong leadership is not afraid to take all feedback on board. Wise leadership gives teams positive and easy to use patterns (like KARA and Team Examen) to elicit the honest and direct feedback in the most positive and engaging manner possible.

Questions for a "Team Leadership" REP

Does your leadership style give everyone a voice? Are <u>V</u>ision, <u>O</u>rganization, <u>I</u>ngenuity, <u>C</u>ollaboration and <u>E</u>ngagement part of your success formula? Have you a KARA and / or a Team Examen type protocol for managing feedback?

<u>Start</u>: Select one idea from the pages above and try it for real when you are ready or feel the need to REP this area.

<u>Evolve</u>: Come back to these pages and ideas from time to time and REP more of the ideas out for real. Maybe at that stage you can decide if you would like to do more of your own research and work on devising your own leadership protocols.

Cultivate Your Leadership Approaches (Models and Practices)

Introduction

"If your actions inspire others to dream more, learn more, do more and become more, you are a leader."

– John Quincy Adams, Sixth President of the United States

Motivation: Why?

This handbook is first about Personal and then Collaborative Leadership and it is obvious that leadership is important to the success of any key undertaking, inside or outside of work. Intuitively I think we all know this, but I wonder do we give the topic of leadership enough focus.

If you manage a team, you really should think about leadership. For example, if you are managing a project, it is very important to have a set of process stages and steps to deliver successful project management, as described in Section 4 of this handbook. This will be your map for collaborative project management, without which you will get lost, your project may fail, and your project team may well be disappointed in you. However, even if you know how to navigate the project management terrain very well, you will need to do so with a leadership style and a set of approaches that works for you as a manager and also works for your project team. In addition, if you are earning your stripes as a first time manager, this may be difficult for you.

The last paragraph is all about you, but what about the members of your team or project? There are numerous studies and surveys showing that large percentages of the workforce are not properly engaged with their company. If you are interested in these surveys, a good place to start is at www.gallup.com. This lack of employee engagement is a sad reality. I say "sad", as I really believe that the vast majority of people would prefer to be fully engaged and enjoying work. We spend so much time at work – all things being equal, who wouldn't want to be happier and more engaged at work?

It seems only right and proper to cultivate a leadership style that encourages higher levels of engagement from all team members. Moreover, in work environments that aspire to be collaboratively managed, higher levels of engagement are vital, not optional. You can and should set the leadership style and tone, and this chapter aims to help you.

The Essence

There are so many definitions of leadership, but I do really like the quote above, that I thought was from John Quincy Adams. The quote articulates well that leadership is all about helping people to get the best out of themselves. What a wonderful and noble aspiration for a leader, to help others be the best that they can be. The fact that the quote was so old gave it a bit more gravitas for me. But, what do you know, he never said this at all! Seems as if the quote, or a version of it, most likely came from Dolly Parton, the singer and entertainer. In any event, I think the quote is a great summary of an extremely positive leadership style and worth using.

Time Out

Have you ever suffered or had to endure bad leadership? On reflection, what did you learn from this experience?
How does your leadership capabilities and style compare to the beautiful quote on the prior page?

It would be good to measure your leadership style from time to time against the quote above. It is a high bar. The rest of this chapter will walk you through ten areas to work to help you develop a collaborative and effective leadership style.

Have Core Values

People willingly follow leaders they like, trust, and respect. If you lose the respect of the team, leadership becomes very difficult, and sometimes too high a hill to climb. This means that the type of person you are and the type of values you live by will affect not only your leadership style but also your leadership success. People will not follow the "do as I say, and not as I do" leader for very long.

What values do you live by? What is your moral compass? Can you go back to your family, faith, or philosophy to identify one? What do you stand for? Does your company have core values that you believe in? Life is short and work is a big part of your short life, so it is better to live by the same good values at work and outside of work. If you decide to be selfish and put yourself first, that is your personal choice, but it will not go down well on collaborative endeavors. You will be found out!

I like these two core values from my work environments:

- Do unto others, as you would have others do unto you.
- Be the change that you wish to see in the world.

In the groups I work with, we could have nominated twenty core values, but choosing two seemed to be a good number, as it gives the two more weight. We have set the expectation that we all work to these core values, not just the managers. In management and in leadership, it is important to set expectations, to set the tone.

The first core value ("do unto others") covers our relationships and interactions with each other, our customers, our partners, our suppliers, and our wider community. It is such a fundamental value that it saves having to define hundreds of other rules and protocols as many actions can be influenced and judged by this one yardstick.

The second core value ("be the change") protects us from complacency and the status quo. It protects us from falling to the low levels of dis-engaged team members. It gives us permission to be the best that we can be. It expects our best and is excited by our best.

As you cultivate your leadership approaches, please be aware that the type of person you are and the way you treat people will greatly influence your ability to be an effective leader. Also be comforted by the fact that the practices in "Section 2 – Personal Leadership" of this handbook will help you lead yourself to a good place. Taking responsibility to lead yourself to a better place, one day at a time, will help you become a strong leader for and with others. Are you personally in that good place already or are you prepared to make the commitment to get there?

Be Mission Focused

As a leader, you need to keep your eye on the mission and the group or project goals. In addition, you need to help people maintain that focus. There is no point being a wonderful and inspiring leader if you are not goal focused! There is no benefit to motivating people if you do not work with them to deliver the goods. Are you mission and objective focused?

Decide on a Leadership Model

You, as a team facilitator or a project manager, are now a leader. If you are managing a team or a project for the first time, then it is like earning your stripes as we used to say in the military. Way back in 1980, in the Army Cadet College, the first Chief of Staff I heard speak told us that the biggest management jump was from Soldier to Corporal (where the first two stripes were earned). It was the jump from no management or leadership responsibility to some. It was the leap from being one of the team members to being in charge of the team.

In the military, there was a strict hierarchy and it was respected, and as a young officer, I had authority as well as responsibility. At the same time, as an officer, I was expected to respect and look after the troops in our Cavalry squadron. Nothing else was acceptable. The troops were expected to follow my lead and I had to look after the troops. Young officers became very comfortable with this apparent contradiction.

In the groups I work with, we have adopted the norm that everyone on the team plays the role of leader for some aspect of the work or project. Everyone on the team is therefore a leader with some given autonomy. The area of work is either a project deliverable or what we call a strategic deliverable. The former is pretty straightforward; it is some key aspect of the given project. The latter, the strategic deliverable, is a key piece of the group strategy for the current year.

So continuing to use my work experience as an example, the CEO (that is me!), the other line managers, and the project managers have a specific leadership responsibility for an area or a project, and every team member has at least one area that they lead for the company or project. The leaders, who are not line managers in the company, thus have the freedom and autonomy to express themselves.

I do not place management on some special pedestal, and I am a senior manager! Don't get me wrong, I see management as a very important aspect of running a project or a company. However, I also see sales, marketing, technical architecture, design, finance, etc. as key skills we need, just as we need management skills. I do, however, put leadership on a very special pedestal. Leadership, from wherever it comes, makes all the difference in the world.

Very few leaders are able to achieve their goals alone, and each leader at our workplace, whether he or she is a line manager or not, is given the authority to:

- set expectations and get agreement on same with a wider team of people (who may or may not be formally on a project)
- give real support to the team
- hold team members accountable for deliverables (as necessary).

I have seen this devolved leadership model work very well. It really helps with both enjoyment and success.

What leadership model is right for your project or situation?

Decide on a Team Model

The last section outlined the leadership model we use in our groups as an example. I do not mean to imply it is the best or only leadership model. Clearly it is neither! However, it is a model that is consistent with Personal and Collaborative Leadership. Continuing to use my work experiences as an example, the next question might well be: "What Team Model do we employ that is also supportive of Personal and Collaborative Leadership?"

Each major team (e.g. engineering, sales, marketing, customer success, etc.) has a General Manager or Vice President (VP). This manager is the leader with overall responsibility to lead and manage the success of that business team. We like to call them teams rather than departments. In addition, each of these teams has sub-teams and so on. Some of the major objectives of these teams require project management to be successful. Each of these projects has a project manager. Teams are formed as needed to deliver on these projects, each with a designated leader. Individuals in the company will be leaders on some teams and serve as team members on other teams. Some teams will be self-managed and self-directed without a formally appointed leader. In this respect, everyone in the company (myself included) plays the role of team member on some teams.

What is the right team model for your project or group?

Decide on Team Dynamics

Because our projects are collaborative, with non-managers playing the role of leaders, we decided it was important to lay out the dynamics of an ideal team as follows.

- Collegiate / Companions (friendly and enjoyable with no need for fear)
- Collaborative (on the one team and on the one project helping each other)
- Challenging (to each other – but respectfully) with the Conflict required for innovation. Be comfortable asking and answering uncomfortable questions
- Can do attitude – and no such thing as I/we can't.

Four Cs of an Ideal Team

Collegiate / Companions   Collaborative   Challenging   Can do attitude

Credit where Credit is Due

A good leader should never claim the work of others as his or hers, so I better fess up! In 2009, the local university MBA class had a leadership lecture from the then Chief of Staff, Lt. Gen. Dermot Earley. I was invited as a local business person, as we recruit from the business studies department of this university. I was also invited as I am ex-Army. The lecture was one of the best I have ever heard on leadership. It was practical and extremely sincere. You just knew that this man lived these principles. Sadly, this great Army General and giant of a man died in 2010 while still serving as

Chief of Staff. A number of the desired leadership and team member practices cited in the next two sections come from that lecture and my prior army officer training, and are marked with an *.

Desired Leadership Practices

As noted above, we have a healthy situation at our place of work in that everyone is a leader for some aspect of work. This is what you aspire to with Personal and Collaborative Leadership. The question then becomes, what is expected of a leader? We found it both necessary and helpful to set these expectations and they are offered here to give you examples of the leadership practices you might like to employ.

- *Integrity is key for leaders. Always treat others as you wish to be treated. Remember one of the two core values from above … *"Do unto others as you would have others do unto you."*
- Lead by example, remembering the other of the two Core Values … *"Be the change that you wish to see in the world"*.
- *Leaders need to create a dream, a vision, a goal and communicate this really well.
- *Leaders need to know themselves and be self-aware. They need to practice what they preach and never bluff.
- *Leaders need to have external awareness and should honestly, empathetically and respectively express:
    - the joy of success, and say "Thanks" more often
    - the pain of failure
    - concern at slow progress.
  In these honest expressions, leaders should empathize with people and all such expressions should be in a calm and controlled manner.
- Delegate Responsibly: The leader cannot and should not carry all. Assign work to people; delegate what you cannot reasonably carry.
- *People are well able for lots of change and will withstand much if everyone gets fair treatment.
- *Always be fair, firm yet friendly – the 3 Fs.
- *Sincere communication is vital. Ask and listen well so you can learn and lead.
- Do not make remarks about the person or personality; rather

focus on the actions, tasks and the job at hand.

- Give very critical and difficult feedback in private and in person in a one-on-one setting – not in the open plan office, not in a group meeting and not on email.
- *Leaders must be visible; they must be seen to be serving with the people they lead.
- *As a new leader you now have weight. Pull your weight – do not throw it around!
- When (not if) an upset or a crisis occurs, do your best to remain cool, calm and collected under pressure and do not start yelling at people. It is easy enough to lead when things are going well. The true measure of a leader is visible in the tough times.
- When (not if!) you breach any of the above desired leadership approaches, be big enough to admit it and apologize at the earliest possible time.

Desired Team Member Practices

In the last few sections, I explained that every person in Personal and Collaborative Leadership plays the role of leader at some point and I called out desired leadership practices. I also explained that everyone on the team (including the manager) plays the role of team member. The next question then becomes, what are the desired practices for the role of team member? Here is a suggested list to get you started, from my work experiences.

- *Integrity is key for all team members. Always treat others as you wish to be treated. Remember one of the two Core Values … *"Do unto others as you would have others do unto you."*
- Assume personal responsibility for the success of the deliverables assigned to you.
- Team effort is the key for greater success. Offer help to the team. Be open and expect new tasks outside your own deliverables.
- *Mistakes happen. Admit and get over them, but learn from them always. Be comfortable to "fall upwards" (as was described in the "Sharpen Your Attitude to Life" chapter). See the later section in this chapter on 'Make the Most of Mistakes'.
- Expect issues from time to time. Deal with them properly and

quickly. Do not let them fester. When the issue is sorted, leave it behind.
- Respect deadlines and sign-off dates for deliverables.
- Work and life is fast-paced at times with multiple, simultaneous commitments, so you will need to periodically invest in time management practices to be able to deliver on your responsibilities.
- *You need the courage as a team member to do the right thing:
  - Take the responsibility given to you and contribute to the team.
  - Challenge the direction and then accept the team direction.
  - Participate in the speed of the group.
  - Take moral actions in line with the two core values.

Situational Leadership: Dictate or Delegate

The leadership techniques and style you deploy will and should depend on the situation at hand. There are several factors that help us understand the situation. Let's look at four:
- Ability Spectrum
  Sometimes you will find the team members capable, competent, and able to do the job at hand. Other times they are on the other end of this spectrum and not capable or trained for the tasks ahead (and many times through no fault of their own).
- Attitude Spectrum
  There will be days when you will find team members energetic, enthusiastic and very willing. Then other days you will find people on the team who are lethargic, lazy, demotivated and could not be bothered.
- Time Pressure Spectrum
  Sometimes there will be no pressure and it will seem like you will have all the time in the world to get a task accomplished and other times it will be very time sensitive or an emergency, with not a second to spare.
- Environment Spectrum
  Some groups live is a very stable and well regulated environment and others live in a manic, high growth, unstable environment, sometimes even in crisis.

It is helpful to plot the above factors on a spectrum, with the left-hand side of the spectrum less desirable than the right side. In most cases as a leader, you will want to do your best to shift the dials to the right.

- On the ability spectrum, you can help people move to the right with more training; people will also get there with time and experience.

- On the attitude spectrum, you can find out what is causing the inertia of the left-hand side and try to deal with these issues and bring the energy to the right hand side.

- On the time spectrum, you can try to buy the team more time to ease the time pressure.

- On the environment spectrum, you can investigate what is causing the chaos that is pushing the dial to the left-hand side and address these issues to move the dial to the calmer right-hand side. But at some stage the situation is as it is, and you have to lead from that point.

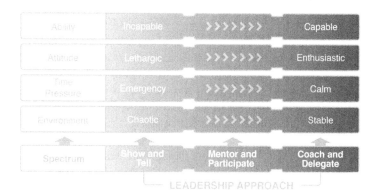

In any of these situations, the practices of leadership described in the prior sections above should remain valid but the approaches you deploy will vary depending on where you are on the spectrum. Let me break these into three leadership approaches:

- Show and Tell

    If you are to the left of some or all of the above spectrums, you will very likely need to show people how to do the task or tell them to just do it. You will not be able to hang about and hope it happens. In this situation, you are giving instructions. The situation can demand you to be somewhat authoritarian, with a positive message and tone. You, of course, will be hoping that this experience will move people more to the right of the spectrum, so your involvement going forward needs to be less invasive.

-   Mentor and Participate

    If you are mid-spectrum on some or all of the above, you will likely help the person understand how to deliver on the task at hand and you may also actively participate as needs be. You are leaving the person with the responsibility, but you are staying close!

-   Coach and Delegate

    If you are to the right of the spectrum, you are typically in a great place. Easy Street! You will be talking to someone about the desired outcome. They will be asking questions and coming up with the first set of answers themselves. You will be there to coach them to the best performance but you will be delegating and by and large leaving it to them.

All three approaches are valid. No one is better than the other. You need to deploy the right approach for the situation you find yourself in.

Manage Poor Performance

Poor performance can come from a number of places. If you look at the four spectrums above, you could imagine poor performance coming from:

-   Low capability: The person is just not able.
-   Low motivation: The person is not bothered.
-   Lack of time: Not enough time given to the job.
-   Chaotic environment: The systems or processes are all wrong or non-existent.

The key is to identify why the performance is poor. If you examine the same four factors and ask "why is this" until you get to the root cause, you might find some of the following to be true:

-   Low capability

    The person was not trained. The person just does not

have the aptitude for this kind of task.
- Low motivation
   The person is not being compensated enough or is suffering a poor manager. The person has a really bad attitude and is displaying aspects of a bad character.
- Lack of time
   The deadline was totally unrealistic. The person completely miscalculated the time needed or planned very poorly.
- Chaotic environment
   The customer keeps changing their mind and is very demanding. The person responsible did not deploy proper and needed systems or processes.

So keep digging until you get to the root cause and reason for the poor performance. At that point, the fix for the poor performance will typically become obvious. If the fix is not yet obvious, you may not yet be at the root cause of the poor performance, so keep investigating. The truth shall set you free! Once you get to the root cause, you will know whether you are in a 'show and tell', a 'mentor and participate' or a 'coach and delegate' situation.

Make the Most of Mistakes

That might seem an odd heading, to 'make the most of mistakes'. It will be entirely possible that you as a leader will feel surprised, let down, frustrated, angry, upset or disappointed that a mistake has occurred. This is an entirely human and is an understandable reaction. The question now becomes, 'what will you do with this emotion?'. You could yell at the person who made the mistake. You might even want to do this! However, you need to ask yourself, 'why are you emotional?' and 'what did you want to happen?' and 'what would you like to happen going forward?'. And, then ask yourself, 'will yelling at the person achieve this desired outcome?'. It is also good to consider if you do 'give out' to the person, are they likely to admit mistakes in the future or try to hide them.

The other side of a mistake is that there is always some lesson to learn, when you understand the root cause of the mistake. It is possible that this mistake will lead to a breakthrough in thinking.

Maybe the person is not fully trained and this needs work. Perhaps the person is lazy and this needs to be addressed. You may find that the process is not adequate for the situation at hand, and this needs attention. You do not wish this mistake to happen again, so you need to find out why it happened in the first place. Ironically, you need your place of work to be a safe place to make and admit mistakes. You want your team to know that mistakes are a source of growth. I was going to title this few paragraphs, 'Grow with Mistakes'.

You may not have worked for a manager that was positive in terms of handling mistakes in the past and you need your own protocol. Here is a constructive protocol you can consider communicating to your team for managing the inevitable and sometimes precious mistakes that will occur from time to time.

- ADMIT: It is OK to make mistakes – we understand – we are human after all. However we are honest enough to acknowledge and admit the mistake. We do not come to work intending to make mistakes. We also know that some (not all!) mistakes will bring fresh opportunities.

- FIX: We make a very serious effort to address the specific mistake – to rectify it soonest – to recover from it quickly. We want to alleviate the effects of this mistake on those who suffer it.

- LEARN/ADJUST/GROW: We also know it is wise to investigate and reflect on mistakes – we need to learn from them – to grow with them. We need to find a way of working that is better going forward that helps avoid the mistakes and that is informed by experience of the mistake. We desire to seek other opportunities that this mistake may uncover – and we want to call these out and enjoy these.

Summary of Cultivate Your Leadership Style

Good leadership is a choice you make. Great leaders are not born thus. Great leaders make the necessary investments. This chapter has lots of ideas and practices that will help you cultivate your own leadership approaches and style.

Questions for a "Team Leadership" REP

Start: Take some time to reflect on the practices above and then select a few to implement when you are ready or feel the need to REP this area. Maybe you REP this for every new project or assignment.

Evolve: Do your own research – the internet is full of great materials and wisdom on Leadership. Invest the time to do the research. Your efforts will be greatly rewarded.

Section 4. Collaborative Project Management

The prior sections focused on personal and situational leadership. If you lead and carry yourself well, and if you can lead various situations well (e.g. meetings, group decisions, presentations) then you are in a good place to take on leading and managing projects.

Introduction to Project Management

If you are in an organization and you want to deliver something new, strategic, exciting, challenging or difficult – it requires a project.

A project is a way to transform, to bring an organization or a group to a new place. A project is a way to realize ambitions. In some cases, a project is a way to help people achieve their dreams.

A project is from here to a new place, to a better place, to an exciting place, to a different place. A project is a way to get to where you want to go.

A really good project should be enjoyable both because of the destination you want to reach and because of the journey you are taking. With a project you should be thinking: "I really want to get there. It is important to me. It is important to my group, or my team, or my organization, and I am enjoying the journey."

Proper project management, exciting project management is both an enjoyable journey and a fabulous destination.

The Essence

There was a time some years back when the workplace was different; some people were very rigidly trained in project management and the other people followed the project leader.

The workforce has changed. By next year, 2020, half the workforce will be millennials. These are people who enter the workforce after the year 2000. There is a lot of very unhealthy and even patronizing commentary on this millennial generation, but by and large, these folks do want to work for a purpose and not a hierarchy. They desire meaningful work. They understand what's happening at work and in society at large. They are willing and able to contribute to the projects. They want to make an impact.

As these smart and energetic people join the workforce, there needs to be a way to tap into the talent of these new recruits who want to help with projects. This is where collaborative project management comes in to play. Collaborative project management is transformed from the old command and control structure – "You'll do what I tell you!" – into, "Let's work together to get this done". I served ten years in the Army, and we were good at the former as the need arose! Modern, effective project management is about collaborative project management. It is people working together, enjoying the journey on the way to an agreed destination.

Time Out

In the next few page we will focus on the reality of too many failed or challenged projects. Before we get there, here are a few questions for you to reflect on:

- Have you personally experienced any challenged or failed projects?

- Have you been connected with a group that has had failed or challenged projects in your current organization? Or, perhaps this happened in your last organization?

It will be worthwhile to take a timeout to think through and reflect on these experiences. Another idea would be to do your own internet research on "failed projects", read the lessons learned, and compare these to your own experiences. We can and should learn from the challenges of others.

Collaborative Project Management – Why?

Why do we need collaborative project management guidance? Surely all projects are running fine and we do not need any help? If you think there might be a need for collaborative resources and guidance, hang with me for a little bit and I will go through some of the main reasons, as to why collaborative project management guidance for any group is probably a good idea.

Traditional Challenges – Failed Projects

You might think because project management is a relatively old and mature discipline, it would be practiced successfully everywhere, and there would not be many failed projects. Unfortunately, this is not the case. What we find is a landscape littered with delayed, challenged, and unfortunately, failed projects. The first two reports below are geographic – the first from Europe and the second from the US. The second two are industry reports from the IT (Information Technology) and Construction sectors.

- "EU wastes migrant aid millions with 'chaotic and badly managed' projects", or so reads the March 17th 2016 headline[3] reporting on a finding by the European Court of Auditors. The report claimed that the projects were poorly designed, badly managed, chaotically supervised and, as a result, were often ineffective. Two-thirds of the 23 projects examined only "partly" met their goals. "This was often due to their excessively vague or general nature, which frequently made it impossible to measure results," the court said.

- The United States Department of Defense canceled 18 major programs in the 2000s, having spent more than $59M, according to a Center for Strategic and International Studies report published in January 2016.[4] The report explains that this money was spent "without any fielded systems to show for it." This data was based on a sample of 18 major programs, so we

---

[3] http://www.telegraph.co.uk/news/worldnews/europe/eu/12196776/EU-wastes-migrant-aid-millions-with-chaotic-and-badly-managed-projects.html
[4] https://csis.org/files/publication/160126_Harrison_DefenseModernization_Web.pdf

assume there were more challenged projects like these. Needless to say, this is a complex topic, but the report does claim that "many of these cancellations were arguably justified due to requirements creep and cost overruns." The report then goes on to explain the other factors, specifically "the cumulative effect of successive acquisition starts, stops, and restarts".

- The Standish Group reported on 50,000 IT projects from around the world in their 2015 Chaos report. In one classification, the report stratifies projects into Successful (29% in 2015), Challenged (52% in 2015) or Failed (19% in 2015).[5]
- According to KPMG's Global Construction survey[6], "Project owners said only 31 percent of their projects came within 10 percent of budget, and just 25 percent within 10 percent of original deadlines, in the past three years" and "Over half of construction project owners experienced one or more underperforming projects in the previous year."

I could have filled more pages with other reports of failed projects, from other geographies and other sectors, but I am sure you get the point. Unfortunately, while we would think that project management is easy and natural, we know that careful and effective project management is non-trivial and is still needed.

Newer Challenges – Collaboration

Ironically as organizations strive for more and more collaboration, it has the tendency in some cases to make project management more challenging. Who would have thought that this would be the case? Let us run through six reasons as to why this can happen:

i. More initiatives in organizations around the world are now delivered, or designed to be delivered, as collaborative projects. Organizations want to complete these projects with a team collaborating well together, sometimes across different offices, countries, time zones, and companies.

---

[5] http://www.infoq.com/articles/standish-chaos-2015

[6] https://home.kpmg.com/xx/en/home/media/press-releases/2015/04/construction-project-failures-weigh-industry.html

ii. Project teams are staffed with intelligent team members from a wide range of backgrounds and disciplines who expect to be involved in the decision making of a project. They are no longer interested in the old 'command and control' type of project management where they were allocated tasks, complete tasks, and did not think too much about their impact on the project.

iii. I am also seeing more and more projects set up with some sort of a project site and / or shared drives, or both. The challenge with some of these projects sites, or shared directories, is that they are often populated with just some, but not all, of the project information. And, you know what they say about a little information being a dangerous thing! It would of course be safer if the project site had all the project information. That way, the extended project team could consider all the information and not just a subset of the project information before forming their opinions, making their decisions and giving their inputs.

iv. Some organizations do have people formally trained in project management, perhaps with models like the Project Management Institute's 'Project Management Body of Knowledge' (PMBOK), or PRINCE2 from the UK. That said, the fourth challenge is we have what a colleague of mine termed the 'P-MBAs' or the 'project managers by accident!'. Often these new project managers are business leads or technically qualified people who, by default, end up leading projects. There is absolutely nothing wrong with technical people leading projects. In fact, it is often a great idea that the person with the most knowledge is in a leadership position. However, many organizations do not spend the time or budget to send these folks on project management training. Hence, they and the project are challenged from the outset.

v. The fifth reason that projects are succumbing to challenges is to do with the so-called 'Millennials' or 'Generation Y'. These are folks born in the 1980s and the 1990s. By and large, this generation, and my own children are among them, have a different set of expectations. They need to be more convinced what they are doing makes sense, is worthwhile, and is for a greater cause or purpose. They are less likely to be involved in something because they were told it was the right thing to do!

vi. The sixth and final reason is that as organizations become more informal and less structured, there is a lack of guidelines and standards for the project managers to follow. Most organizations I encounter do not have a defined process or set of standards to guide new project managers. You might say this does not really matter – and in some cases, you may be right – but what if an organization wants to move people around to drive larger projects to success? Some common ways of managing projects would be useful. Similarly, what if an organization has problems delivering projects with these new project managers? Would it not be better to have a project management process to fix rather than a person to blame?

Look at these six trends above and put yourself in the shoes of new project managers. You will see it is somewhat challenging in this environment for new project managers to collaboratively manage projects and bring them home successfully.

Embrace the Change

A little earlier, I explained that it has always been difficult to manage projects. I called these the traditional challenges of the failed or challenged projects. Above I covered six newer challenges that face today's project managers. When we look at some of these newer challenges, we also find a wonderful new opportunity. When turned around, these challenges become possibilities to manage projects in a very different way. If some very smart people are willing and ready to help manage your project to success, and if modern collaborative tools are coming on stream, why not take advantage of these new possibilities? It makes a lot of sense not to fight these challenges, but to embrace them.

Do you need Project Management Guidance?

It is possible to carry out a simple four question self-test to see if your group needs collaborative project management guidance.

i. Projects meeting expectations?
    "Are all your projects performing to expectations and are they delivering the results your customers expect?" If the answer to this question is yes, then you have absolutely nothing to worry about. If the answer is no, you should probably proceed to question two!

ii. Visibility into projects?
    "Can you at least get real time visibility into these projects?" If the

projects are not running the way you wish, then you should at least be able to see what is going on in the projects so you can take the appropriate actions. If you answer yes to this question, you are probably in good shape. However, if you answer no, you should probably keep going to question three!

iii. Trained project teams?

"If you can't see into what's happening on the projects, are all the people involved in the projects skilled and trained in project management or collaborative project management?" If they are all trained and skilled, then you probably have very little to worry about. However, if they are not, then you probably should proceed to question four.

iv. Local guidance available?

"What if the projects aren't working the way you wish, you can't see into the projects and the people don't have deep training in project management, is there at least local guidance and are there templates available on how to deliver projects collaboratively?"

If you answer no to the above four questions, then it probably makes sense to develop or find some local collaborative project management guidance, and this handbook should help.

Time Out

At the very start of this handbook, I quoted from Aristotle: *"That which we learn to do we learn by doing."* Our challenge is to find time so that we can change, improve or evolve how we manage projects. With all of this in mind, the "Start|Evolve" approach to implementing the learnings of this handbook will help.

<u>Start</u>: Ask yourself the four question self-test above. Then you can decide if your investment in collaborative project management guidance is needed either now or later. Answering questions about "why" change is needed is a critical step in the process.

<u>Evolve</u>: Later, you might ask your leadership team to take the four question self-test. This will hopefully prompt a discussion to see if an investment in a collaborative project management process is necessary or justified for your wider group.

Collaborative Project Management – What?

Introduction

This chapter will explain an approach to project management that is influenced by and very aware of the enemies that conspire to make successful project management challenging and difficult. First, we need to have a shared view of what constitutes a project.

Characteristics of a Project

How do you know you have a project on your hands? Here follows six common characteristics of a project that help answer this question:

i. A project is often for a designated customer or customer base.
ii. A project is temporary in nature. It typically has a defined start and a defined end. At least it has an ideal or target end.
iii. A project will have a unique and specific set of objectives that need to be delivered within the boundaries of the project.
iv. A project is typically more of a once-off endeavor rather than something that is happening all the time in a repeated fashion.
v. A project is not 'business as usual', which is more akin to a process.
vi. A project can be cross-functional, or indeed cross-organizational.

Project Management Definitions

The PMI (Project Management Institute) has established standards for Project Management. These standards are incorporated into PMBOK and define a project as:

- A job that has a beginning and an end (Time)
- At a stated level of Performance (Quality)
- At a budget (Cost) and a specific outcome (Scope).

PRINCE2 (a process that originated in the UK) defines standard approaches to project management as: *"a temporary organization that is created for the purpose of delivering one or more business products according to an agreed business case."*

Project Constraints

You will also find that your project can be described by multiple conflicting constraints. Here are five of the most common-place and typical constraints:

i. Scope: The scope defines the customer's needs and the requirements expressed and implied.

ii. Time: Typically, a project is required by a customer in a fixed amount of time and by a deadline.

iii. Quality: The third constraint is the quality of the work required on the project. To what standard is the project expected to deliver?

iv. Cost/Resources: The fourth constraint is the amount of money, budget or resources that are available to be expended on the project.

v. Value: Another constraint is the amount of value provided by the project or this iteration of the project.

It is obviously not possible to fix and agree on all five of these constraints as the projects starts, which is why they are called conflicting constraints. Let us take a simple example to explain. As you start a new project, it is unlikely that you can agree to deliver forty new requirements on your project, in one year, to a perfect quality standard, with one person on the team and deliver all the business value expected. Why not? You probably do not know enough about the specifics of the requirements. You do not yet know what else might happen in the year. It is likely that there is no common understanding of what the quality standard is to be able to make this commitment.

Given this, it is important to listen to your customer and ask enough questions so you understand which of these constraints are really critical and therefore fixed. Is it that all the requirements must be delivered? Alternatively, is something significant needed by the end of the year, even if not all the requirements are delivered to deliver a specific value to the customer? On the other hand, is it that you need to do as much as you can with four people and a hundred thousand dollars? This is often called the time–quality–cost triangle.

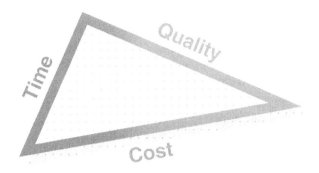

Time, quality and cost are the three sides of the triangle, representing the constraints and you need to elongate or shorten each of the sides so they continue to form a triangle and are in balance. You may be fixing one of the constraints (e.g. time) and adjusting the other two to match. The above diagram is typical of how the challenge of constraints is represented. However, there are usually more than three constraints and therefore your triangle becomes a rectangle or a pentagon, etc.

Let me use an example close to home. In one of our groups, we now release a new product to our customers every quarter, so we fix the time constraint at three months. The quality and the ease of use has to meet a very high standard, as it is not acceptable to ship poor quality software. In this case, the time and the quality are both fixed and therefore the third constraint, which is the value and scope of functionality we deliver, is the one that varies. We try to fit in as much useful capability as we can in each quarterly release, but we have decided that it has to be delivered in a fixed amount of time and with a very high degree of quality. In our case, time and quality are fixed and the project scope is variable. Sometimes we deliver more value than originally planned and sometimes we deliver less.

An Ideal Approach to Project Management

In an ideal world, we would be able to manage projects using the following simple process with four stages:

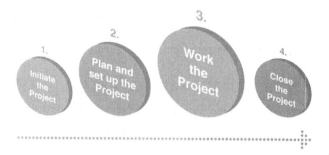

The Enemies of Project Management

As we know, we do not live in an ideal world! There is a wonderful old quote from a Prussian Army Chief of Staff that can be paraphrased as follows: *"No plan ever survives the first encounter with the enemy."* (Helmuth Karl Bernhard Graf von Molted (1800 – 1891), Chief of Staff of the Prussian Army and Master Strategist).

When we say that no plan ever survives the first encounter with the enemy, we should probably identify the enemies! There are at least five enemies conspiring and getting ready to derail your project and I am sure you could add another few yourself.

i. Project Constraints: You know a project has to deliver on time, to a high level of quality within some defined cost parameters, and to some agreed scope. It can be very difficult for a project manager to keep these constraints in balance. This reality is challenging to say the least.

ii. Poor Planning: Poor estimation or poor planning can doom a project from the start. This can often happen due to a lack of time or lack of experience on behalf of the project manager.

iii. Issues: Actual problems or issues occur on pretty much every project. There is no escaping them. They happen. They are real.

iv. Risks: Another challenge are the risks that might come to pass. These distract us, as we need to keep an eye on them, and some of these we need to mitigate against.

v. Change Requests: The fifth enemy that conspires to derail the initial plan are the inevitable set of change requests, formal or informal, that arise on projects.

These so-called enemies are the normal stuff of project management. This is what a project manager is trained to expect to have to contend and deal with. Because these enemies are very real, an ideal approach to project management is not possible.

A Real Project Management Approach

In order to successfully manage a project, you need an approach. You may choose to call this a process or standard but we will not get too bureaucratic with terminology in this handbook! A very real yet simple approach to collaborative project management is based on the ideal approach explained above and is aware of the realities of project management. The resulting approach is then comprised of the following five stages:

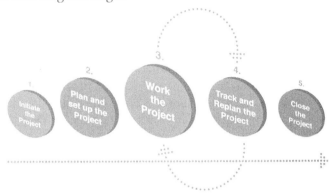

The process of re-planning is a constant one, since in reality and by necessity project plans do change, which is why we add the new fourth stage, "Track and Re-plan the Project." We will explore the five stages in more detail in the rest of this Section 4.

A Collaborative Approach to Project Management

The practices of collaborative project management enable individuals from different departments, offices, companies, and even countries, to collaborate and successfully deliver a project. These practices help all team members fully engage to contribute in a positive and meaningful way to a successful project outcome. Critically, the practices also provide guidance and processes for new and 'accidental or occasional project managers' who lack formal project management training. In a project that is managed collaboratively, the team will plan the project together, act together and track the project together.

- **Plan Together**: It is best to have the team who will deliver the project involved in planning. The quality of the resulting plan will be better and the engagement of all team members will be higher. This is probably common sense to most of us, but we know that common sense is not that common!

- **Act Together**: It is very desirable to have the team act in unison on the project. We all want our project teams to know what is happening and to know what they have to do to ensure project success. If the team is not acting well together, for whatever reason, as a project manager you need to take action.

- **Track Together**: The extended team (project manager, team members, senior executives, customers, etc.) will need to know what is and is not happening on the project in order to constructively contribute to the project outcome.

Time Out

At this stage, take a short time out. Take a few moments to think about the ideas just covered and ask yourself the following questions:
- What projects are underway in your group?
- What work is underway in your group that you might now classify as a project?
- Which of these projects could you use to sharpen your collaborative project management trade?

Portfolio Management

It is not uncommon for people to be confused by terminology, such as project management and portfolio management. A larger project, or perhaps the implementation of some organizational goal or strategy, will often require more than one project. When you get involved in a collection of projects, you may encounter any one of the following terms: portfolio, project portfolio, project office, or

PMO. The PMO refers to the "project management office" or is sometimes called the "program management office."

You will also see a hierarchy of project management constructs and terms that go as follows: project at the bottom, rolling to a program above, rolling up to a portfolio. There is no right and wrong use of the preceding terms or phrases. In your group, I assume that you have many, many projects and use some of this terminology. Typically, it is best to ask locally how the terms are used and in what context.

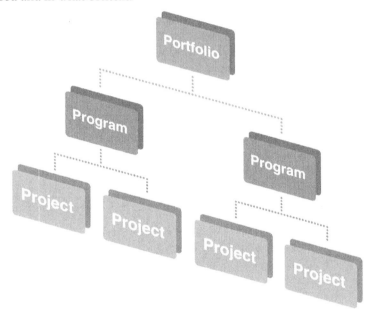

The Collaborative Tool Assumption

This handbook assumes that you wish to manage the project collaboratively with your team. It also assumes that you have access to some collaborative platform, e.g. Microsoft SharePoint. The collaborative platform does not have to be SharePoint, but this is a very popular tool set. According to the Microsoft website in February 2019, "*more than 200,000 organizations and 190 million people have SharePoint for intranets, team sites and content management.*"

SharePoint has delivered a free version since the year 2000, so the availability of SharePoint or something 'SharePoint-like' is not too big an assumption these days. SharePoint 2013 Foundation was the last free version of SharePoint delivered and is an amazing product given its free price point! The newer versions, SharePoint 2016 and SharePoint 2019, do not deliver a free Foundation version.

You might ask the question – is this Section 4 of the handbook about collaboratively managing projects or perhaps more about managing projects on SharePoint? It is absolutely about the former, collaborative project management. However, we just cannot imagine managing a project without some shared project space – hence the few (but not too many) SharePoint references you will find in this section of the handbook. If you have a different collaborative platform and toolset, that is just great.

Questions for a "Collaborative Project Management" REP

Start: When you are ready or feel the need to REP this area, investigate if there is a collaborative project management process defined in your organization. If there is one, you could study it. If there is no such process, you might study how actual projects are delivered and understand and perhaps map this.

Evolve: Most organizations do not have a defined common approach or collaborative toolset for project management, so do not feel alone if this is the case in your organization. If you wish to evolve, one suggestion is to ask your colleagues and managers why there is not a collaborative management process/toolset, and then see where this exploration takes you and the team.

Get a Fast Start – Track Projects

Introduction

This chapter outlines how you can easily track projects before you start fully managing them. This, in turn, ironically will help you manage the projects, when the timing is right!

"The secret of getting ahead is getting started."

— Mark Twain

The Essence

Why begin with merely tracking projects? Many groups are not ready for full collaborative project management and some projects are too small to get the complete treatment. What do you track? Just track the high level project details. This is the kind of project information that is probably floating around on an Excel file. But this chapter suggests you do this with a little bit more style, ease, and substance!

Time Out

Do you see a need for this kind of simple project tracking and do you have a satisfactory mechanism to do so?

Why Only Project Tracking?

Why would we resort to, or maybe start with, tracking projects rather than fully managing projects? Well there are at least two reasons. Firstly, the project might be quite small, or is a project you find very easy to deliver as you have done it many times before. In these scenarios, it does not make sense to deploy a very large amount of project management. The second reason is you and the team may not be ready to use a large amount of collaborative project management. This can be the case even when the project deserves and needs lots of project management. This could be due to a lack of experience, a lack of time, a lack of budget, lack of appetite; whatever the reason the team is just not ready for large amounts of project management. This can be a tough but honest call to make. In both of these cases, it seems wise to start with project tracking and to do that extremely well. This is an important first step towards collaborative project management. And, as we know, all successful journeys being with the first few steps.

A Project Management Spectrum

| ULTRA-LITE | LITE | STANDARD | STRUCTURED |

If you believe what the last few paragraphs were saying, this implies a need for differing amounts of project management. In this simple example of a practical project management spectrum, there are four sections. The sections go left to right, from Ultra-Lite to Lite to Standard and to Structured, depicting different and increasing amounts of project management. You will note that there are arrows on both ends of the spectrum. This reflects the fact that even though you start in one place, for example Lite, you might move left to Ultra-Lite at a later point or you may move right on the spectrum toward Standard. This reflects the reality that different projects require differing amounts of project management at different times.

Time Out

- Where are your projects on this project management spectrum? (i.e., how much project management are they receiving in reality?)
- Where do you think your projects should be on this spectrum? (i.e., how much project management do they need?)

I have found this spectrum very honest and extremely real. The next chapter, 'Initiate the Project', offers more details on choosing the level of project management needed.

A Natural Order

A natural companion to the project management spectrum is the aforementioned "Start|Evolve" approach. Many organizations successfully start with a reasonable and modest amount of project management, to give teams immediate visibility into what's going on, by tracking the projects. Once a project team has visibility into where the project is, it is then possible to decide what levels of control to exert going forward. This will enable the team to gradually evolve, improve and mature their project management practices with a high degree of flexibility. This is reminiscent of the agile approach to project delivery, which advocates delivering a little and often, so that real-world feedback can be early and frequent.

Suggestion: Track the Essentials

Starting with the Ultra-Lite side of the project management spectrum, you can track the essentials of the project. These might include:

- Project name
- Project manager
- Type of project
- Customer or department that the project is for
- Required finish date from the customer
- Likely finish date based on the current progress
- Overall health of the project, as determined by the project manager
- And lastly, project status. Is this project in trouble?

Just tracking these essential key items and reporting on them, even if it's only to yourself, will help you better manage the project. If you track and report these items to the other stakeholders in the project, the team members, senior management and the customer, you will inevitably get feedback to better manage the project. It is not that the other items like tasks, issues, risks, and change requests are not happening; it is that they are not formally tracked in a consistent, central, and transparent manner. Here we are suggesting that you begin by more formally tracking the essentials.

If you can't beat them join them!

If I were to ask you "what are the most common project management tools in use in your organization", you might well reply some combination of Microsoft Excel and Microsoft Outlook. It makes sense that these are in widespread use for project management because they are so easy to use. You will often see a status report typed into an Excel file and sent around on email. While these Excel project status files have many advantages, they also have many disadvantages. Can you tell if the Excel file you are looking at is the latest version? Maybe you are not sure who updated it and when it was last updated. You are not sure if there are other Excel files are floating around. Are other people looking at a different version of the file and making decisions based on this? There is also the disadvantage that multiple people cannot safely make updates at the same time. Nevertheless, despite the disadvantages, the ease of use makes Excel arguably the most popular project management tracking tool on the planet. As they say, if you can't beat them, why not join them!

Use Excel inside SharePoint

Many organizations will use a Projects Tracker inside of SharePoint that mimics the ease of use of Microsoft Excel. With this Projects Tracker approach, you can track the essentials of the project in a grid that looks and acts like Microsoft Excel.

Project ID		Priority	Project Status	Health Indicator	Time Indicator	Cost Indicator	Quality Indicator	% Complete
☐	Systems Projects	High	In Progress	Green	Red	Yellow	Green	75%
☐	Upgrade Hardware	Normal	In Progress	Green	Green	Green	Green	10%
☐	Install New OS	High	In Progress	Green	Red	Yellow	Green	35%
☐	Training for Finance Dept	Normal	In Progress	Green	Green	Green	Green	5%
☐	Hardware Inventory	Normal	In Progress	Green	Red	Green	Yellow	10%
☐	Setup Server Farm	High	In Progress	Red	Green	Green	Green	50%

This approach has many advantages. There is now a single source of project truth. The tracker is as easy to use as Microsoft Excel in its grid style and shape. It also has a version history and an audit trail, so you can go back to prior versions and see who made what changes to the project status and when. In this instance, you are not in the Excel hell that can sometimes happen with project tracking.

The other advantage is that when you save work on this tracker, it can transform into a dashboard, which is more attractive and looks the way people would expect a project management dashboard to appear.

Projects Tracker

!	☐	Health	Time	Cost	Quality	Project Link ID	% Complete	Start Date	Finish Date
!	▶	✓	✗	ⓘ	✓	Systems Projects	75%	3/20/2016	9/20/2016
	▶	✓	✓	✓	✓	Upgrade Hardware	10%	3/20/2016	8/20/2016
!	▶	✓	✗	ⓘ	✓	Install New OS	35%	3/21/2016	12/10/2016
	▶	✓	✓	✓	✓	Training for Finance Dept	5%	3/22/2016	9/23/2016
	▶	✓	✗	✓	ⓘ	Hardware Inventory	10%	3/23/2016	4/21/2016
!	▶	✗	✓	✓	✓	Setup Server Farm	50%	3/24/2016	6/25/2016

Traffic lights icons and high priority signs are depicted graphically. You can see multiple projects in one place and click to get more detail. You can also click to get the version history associated with this project. You are essentially getting the benefits of Excel in terms of ease of use without the associated disadvantages that are present for project tracking.

If you subscribe to this project spectrum approach for any of the aforementioned reasons, then why not use a Projects Tracker inside of SharePoint in the same manner as you use Excel? It is a great way to get many projects reported and get project management started in a consistent manner. It gives a quick win without a lot of fuss. If your organization is currently submitting project updates on Excel, it is an easy transition to make.

Summary of Track Projects

If you start on the left hand side of the spectrum in an Ultra-Lite way and you are tracking the essentials of a project, you can then move more easily to the right hand side into a Lite way and start adding in work items for your projects such as tasks or deliverables or even issues.

You get the quick start via projects tracking with the option to add in the tracking of work items on the project. This way, you get both project and work tracking. This is a very easy transition for people to make in an organization.

The key point to remember is by tracking these key items about your project and reporting on them, even if it is only to yourself, you and the rest of the team will better manage the project. It is an effective and easy start on the road to collaborative project management.

Questions for a "Project Tracking" REP

<u>Start</u>: When you are ready or feel the need to REP this area, check if some of the projects in your group are such that a simple tracker will suffice and maybe start to practice "managing" projects this way, even if just reporting to yourself.

<u>Evolve</u>: Offer to develop a standard tracker for your group and get it approved. You could then get other managers and departments to use this new tracker with everybody singing off the same hymn sheet as they say. Projects visibility would then be greatly enhanced.

Stage 1 – Initiate the Project

Introduction

This chapter will walk you through the first of the five stages of collaborative project management: Initiation.

"A journey of a thousand miles must begin with a single step."
— Lao-Tzu (604-531 BC), Chinese Philosopher

The Essence

Why would you be interested in formally initiating a project? Well, fools rush in! As a project manager, you want to know what you are getting before you officially start. At this stage, you need to secure resources for the project and ideally enlist the support of a project sponsor.

Time Out

- How do you initiate new projects?
- Is this the same way that everyone else in your group initiates projects? Or, are there other methods in practice?

Initiate the Project in 3 Steps

This handbook breaks each of the five stages of Collaborative Project Management into three steps labelled A, B and C. The Initiate stage is about starting the project using these three steps:

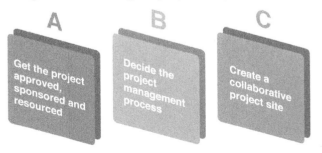

A — Get the project approved, sponsored and resourced

B — Decide the project management process

C — Create a collaborative project site

Forgiveness or Permission!

Sometimes it is easier to ask for forgiveness than seek permission, and there are certainly times that this is very true. However, when initiating new projects, this is not typically the case. Ask for permission to initiate the project so that you have the resources, and more importantly, the sponsorship lined up in your favor. There are many times on the project that you will be able to crash through the barriers yourself. However, every now and again you will need the project sponsor to help you deal with tough situations or make difficult decisions. Now is the time to put that sponsorship in place.

Of course, the other reason to ask for permission to start the project is as a professional courtesy. You owe it to your management team and sponsors to let them know that you are committing resources by starting a new project in the organization.

A. Get the Project Approved, Sponsored and Resourced

The first step is to get the project approved, sponsored and resourced. A good question to ask is what might you need for this step? Be careful in your selection of the project sponsor, if you have a choice. You want someone who can advocate, who cares about the project and who has the time to give the project. This maybe the most senior mat be. It is very likely that you will at least need a face-to-face meeting with the project sponsor. It is also possible that the sponsor will request a written project proposal, a project charter / statement. Even if the sponsor does not request one, it is a good idea to produce one for yourself and the rest of the project team.

A project charter or statement will typically contain some of the following kind of information:

- Project identification
- Project description
- Project objectives, goals, deliverables
- Resources and budget needed
- Priority of the project
- Organization/customer that the project is for
- Proposed project manager

- Type of the project
- Status of the project
- When the project should start and finish
- Any other assumptions about the project.

Certain projects will also require a high-level plan at this early stage. The amount of information and process needed for this first step will depend on the project in hand, the organization you are working for, and the preferences of the project sponsor you are trying to sign up.

The sponsor will ultimately decide if the project is going to go ahead or will bring you in front of the people that can make this determination. The sponsor should also be able to allocate the people you need to work on the project and free up any other resources such as budget. During the process, you have also started to work and collaborate with your project sponsor, which is a very important relationship for you to have. From time to time, you will need this air cover. The ideal minimum exit criteria from this step is that you have secured approval and sponsorship.

You have now taken the first step as a new project manager. Congratulations on having started the journey.

B. Decide the Project Management Process

As they say, be careful what you ask for, you just might get it! Once the project is approved, you need to decide how to manage the project and how much project management rigor you will apply. As depicted in the sample spectrum below, some projects require a lighter touch and some require much more project management.

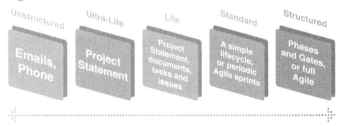

- Unstructured: You manage using phone calls and emails.
- Ultra-Lite: A project definition in the form of a project

statement is agreed and guides the project.
- Lite: You use tasks, issues and documents to manage the project to deliver on the agreed project statement.
- Standard: You deploy a simple lifecycle of tasks in waterfall manner, or you use a basic version of Agile with periodic sprints.
- Structured: You elect to use a stricter lifecycle of tasks and deliverables with phases, gates, and change requests. Or maybe you elect to deploy the full Agile approach with all the ceremonies (i.e. backlog, sprints, sprint planning, estimation, retrospectives, etc.)

This handbook will explain a little more on Waterfall and Agile in the next chapter called, 'Stage 2 – Plan and Setup the Project'.

Your organization may have guidelines or templates for different project types, which will make this step simpler, as you will be selecting a pre-defined approach and then perhaps tailoring it. This will make your life easier as long as the local guidelines are sensible! We have found that sometimes organizations expect way too much project management. In some of these cases, the project manager is not experienced enough to utilize this larger amount of project management. In other cases, the amount of project management is simply too large for the type of project at hand.

The outcome of this step may also have been determined by the prior approval step, if your hands-on project sponsor gave you a process to follow.

If you do not have local guidance, use this step to think through the typical project management items and decide which ones you need to assist you to manage your project. Typical items include:
- Project Statement / Project Definition / Project Charter
- Goals
- Resources and budget needed
- Teams, Roles and Responsibility Definition
- Tasks
- Work Breakdown Structure (for Waterfall projects)
- Backlog, Sprints and Iterations (for Agile projects)
- Documents / Deliverables
- Issues
- Risks
- Contacts
- Decisions

- Change Request Documents
- Actions / To Do List
- Meetings (Agenda, Minutes and Actions)
- Status Reports
- Communications
- Conversations
- Processes and Procedures
- Lessons Learned.

This is not a definitive list but a good one to get you thinking. Here you are deciding what project management you will sign up for and what you will make transparent to the project team. For example, you might decide to track issues in a list but not to manage risks formally. However, this does not mean you will not naturally carry out risk management. You will probably consider and take actions to mitigate risks in your own mind but you are not committing to document or communicate these actions. You may also find that some of these items will have been prepared or at least started for the Project Approval in the prior step.

C. Create a Collaborative Project Site

This handbook assumes a collaborative project management approach. It supposes you are acting as a project manager and not as a project dictator. It assumes you want team members and stakeholders to know what has happened and what needs to happen, so they are empowered to help you deliver and manage the project. This handbook also presumes that you want to setup a collaborative site to share this information.

There are so many free collaborative site options available today that this is no longer a big assumption. I started using Vax Notes when I worked with Digital back in 1990, moved to Lotus Notes in 1995 for my projects and then started using SharePoint in 2000. Microsoft SharePoint 2013 still has a free version, Microsoft SharePoint Foundation, so you have no excuses! Get collaborative in your project management approach with SharePoint or whatever platform you find suitable.

The site you set up needs to mirror the approach to project management that you will undertake. Below is a table depicting some templates to jumpstart your ideas. For example, on the left you are following a lite approach and managing with a few elements, e.g. Project Statement, Issues, and Tasks. On the right, you are following a structured approach and managing everything you can think of! You can start out with one approach at the outset and later evolve as project needs dictate.

Lite	Standard	Structured
Project Home	Project Home	Project Home
Project Help	Project Help	Project Help
Initiate & Plan	Initiate	Initiate
Project Statement	Project Statement	Project Statement
Tasks Update	Goals	Goals
Task Reports	Contacts	Contacts
Documents	Plan	Plan
Execute & Control	Tasks Update	Tasks Update
My Work Reports	Task Reports	Task Reports
Work Reports	Documents	Documents
Issues Update	Risks	Teams & Roles
Issue Reports	Resource Reports	Risks
Status Reporting	Execute	Resource Reports
Site Contents	My Work Reports	Execute
	Work Reports	My Work Reports
	Discussions	Work Reports
	Control	Discussions
	Issues Update	Email
	Issue Reports	Wiki
	Metrics	Control
	Status Reporting	Issues Update
	Site Contents	Issue Reports
		Metrics
		Status Reporting
		Change Requests
		Close
		Lessons Learned
		Post Mortem
		Site Contents

Questions for a "Project Initiation" REP

<u>Start</u>: Apply some of this guidance to your current project, when you are ready or feel the need to REP this area. Maybe you deploy a collaborative site? Perhaps you go look for a project sponsor? Even if the project has started, it is never too late.

<u>Evolve</u>: Use the guidance in this chapter to REP on your next project, or perhaps recommend it to some of your colleagues for their projects.

Stage 2 – Plan and Setup the Project

Introduction

This chapter will guide you through the steps to plan your project, ideally collaboratively with your (new) project team.

> *"In all things, success depends upon previous preparation, and without such preparation there is sure to be failure."*
>
> – *Confucius (c550 – c478 BC) Chinese Philosopher*

The Essence

As they say, failing to plan is planning to fail. At this stage, you wish to plan collaboratively the main steps of the project with the team.

Time Out

Now is a good opportunity for a short time out to give you a chance to get your head into what we are about to discuss. A few questions for you to do just this:

- How do you plan new projects today?
- Is this the way everybody else in your group plans projects? Alternatively, are there different processes in practice?

Plan and Setup the Project

As you enter this stage, your project is approved and you have already decided how to manage the project, or at least you have an outline approach. Hopefully, you have also set up a collaborative site. Now it is time to earn your stripes, and plan and set up your project. You should find the following three steps helpful for this second stage of collaborative project management:

A. Plan the Project
B. Desk Check the Project Plan
C. Notify the Team of their Responsibilities.

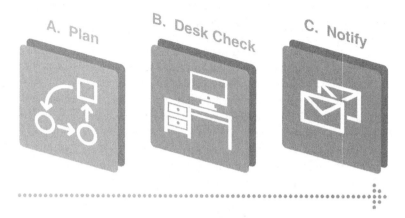

Planning – How Collaborative?

The question at this stage is how collaborative can or should your planning be? How much should you involve your team in planning the project? You have at least three options.

The first option is to bring the team together to execute the aforementioned three steps. As a team, plan the project in a workshop. Desk check the resulting project plan, again in a workshop. Then you can easily notify relevant individuals of their responsibilities because they are with you in that same planning workshop.

The second option is to do all the planning work yourself before bringing the team together to notify them of their responsibilities.

The third option is to do a mix of the above two. In this case you do a chunk of the initial planning for the new project and then bring in the team to help finish out the planning.

The first option, collaboratively working through the three steps, is preferable. It requires more up front time, but has the potential to save you time in the long run. If collaborative planning is well executed, you will get a better result, i.e. a better plan. It will certainly generate more understanding and buy in from your project team.

It may be obvious which approach will work best for your project. If you are finding it difficult to choose, you may find the earlier chapter 'Make Good Decisions' useful.

In summary, it is key to involve team members as much as possible in the project setup and planning.

Planning – Waterfall or Agile

Some projects deploy a simple task list and other more involved projects have tasks organized into a lifecycle of phases. This method of project management, often labelled Waterfall, has been successful for generations, when practiced well. The method is called Waterfall, as it evokes the image of water falling from on high to a lower point and not going backwards. However, practitioners of this Waterfall approach always go back and retrace their steps, willingly and unwillingly! They retrace unwillingly when they find a problem and have to rework that which was thought to be done. They retrace willingly when they anticipate a problem or a new need or issue arises and they adjust the plans. While Waterfall is a commonly accepted image for this style of project management – like many images it is a helpful but imperfect depiction of what happens in reality.

In recent years an Agile rather than a Waterfall / lifecycle approach has been much advocated and has also been very successful. Here are a few pointers to explain the essence of Agile. To begin, I find these three principles to be instructive, as they help explain and guide Agile implementations:

- Incremental Deliveries

    Deliver small amounts of the project or deliverable sooner rather than later. Do not wait for the entire project to be complete before delivering.

- Frequent Feedback

    Setup mechanisms where you can listen to and get feedback from the stakeholders. As you might imagine, it is easier for the stakeholders to give feedback if they are looking at incremental deliveries. These interactions will be a great teacher.

- Build Trust

    A true agile project requires good trust between your team and the customer. Build this trust as you proceed through the project. It is very important.

The following three practices are practical ways to deliver on the three principles above and are key ingredients of Agile:

- Sprints

    Agree weekly, bi-weekly, monthly or quarterly sprints

where key deliverables are produced.
- Backlog
  Have a prioritized backlog for the as-not-yet planned deliverables. This can serve to highlight the opportunity waiting.
- Reviews
  Relook at the progress, the sprints and backlogs on a periodic basis.

A. Plan the Project

The thinking in this handbook is that, at a minimum, you will need a Project Definition/Statement and also a task list (of some sort) on most projects. Additional artifacts (e.g. issues, risks, etc.) should have been nominated for inclusion in the Initiation Stage of the project (unless you skipped this stage!). Four sub-steps to plan the project are as follows:

  i. Complete the Project Statement
  ii. Define and Allocate the Tasks
  iii. Add the Other Project Artifacts Needed
  iv. Assign the Work.

i. Complete the Project Statement

The Project Statement is also known by other names, such as the Project Profile, Project Charter, or Project Definition. This is the master project document, which communicates the intention of the project and other high-level information. In this document, you will want to make very clear what the goal of the project is. It is important for all involved to know where the finish line is. Some of this Project Statement information (e.g. status, scheduled finish date, etc.) is updated throughout the course of the project. In many cases, Project Statement information is used to collate project status reports as the project progresses. The Project Statement that you are completing here was likely started in the 'Project Initiation' stage, as described in the prior chapter.

ii. Define and Allocate Tasks

Sometimes you will know upfront how to organize and deliver the tasks on your project. It might be a simple task list or maybe a waterfall with phases and gates or perhaps an agile approach to delivery. If you are unsure at this juncture, it is good to have a brainstorm of the tasks needed to complete the project successfully or at least the tasks you know about at this stage. Once you have an initial list of tasks, you can then start to organize them. Here are three possible variations:

- Flat Task List: It is possible that a simple and flat task list will suffice, with no other organization of the tasks.
- Lifecycle: Sometimes you will decide to organize your project by work packages, key deliverables, or you may follow a lifecycle (e.g. a waterfall software development lifecycle or a waterfall new product introduction lifecycle). The lifecycle decision will dictate the tasks needed and the manner in which they are organized. In this case you will typically elect to use a WBS (work breakdown structure) that has parent and sub-tasks, and dependencies between tasks (i.e. some tasks cannot start until other tasks finish).
- Agile: Perhaps you desire to run an agile project with many sprints, each lasting a fixed period (e.g. two weeks), and each striving to deliver a piece of the project. This Agile decision will in turn dictate the tasks needed and the manner in which they are organized. In this case you will need a way to manage a backlog of items, and you will also manage tasks within sprints.

No matter which approach you elect to deploy on your project, you will need to have a place and a way to manage the resulting tasks. At this stage, you may also elect to use a simple SharePoint task list or perhaps Microsoft Project to draw up the task list and assignments if you are working with a WBS.

If you use Microsoft Project to create your WBS, you should be aware that Microsoft SharePoint and Microsoft Project Professional have very tight integration with a two-way sync feature.

iii. Add Other Project Artifacts

Once you have defined your Project Statement and project tasks, you now move to generate any extra artifacts required to manage your project. If you are lucky enough to have local guidance, you can use these templates. If you are really lucky, you can create the artifacts using templates pre-loaded in your collaborative site.

Candidate artifacts include goals, documents, issues, risks, etc. In essence, these are the project management sub-processes for your project. Ideally, the type of artifacts required will have been decided in the second step (Decide the Project Management Process) of the prior Initiate stage.

iv. Assign the Work

I have seen some project managers delegate all or most the work on the project and not take their fair share of the load. This is not right. Other project managers tend to do more work on the project than they need to and often find it difficult to delegate. Given that we are talking about collaborative project management, it is especially important to remember that the project work can and should be delegated.

> *"The way to get things done is not to mind who gets the credit*
> *for doing them."*
> *– Benjamin Jowett (1817 – 1893) English scholar, essayist and priest*

If your project is simple with a small team, you will know who is free and not free. In this case, you will assign the tasks and artifacts to your team members as you create them in the prior two steps ("Define and Allocate Tasks" and "Assign the Work").

Some organizations have a more formal definition of roles in use. In this case, you will likely assign a generic role (e.g. business analyst, financial analyst, customer tester, etc.) to a task or artifact in the preceding two steps. You will later assign a person in place of these generic roles. Using a project site with a list of tasks and artifacts with generic pre-assigned roles is a quick way to set up a new project. All you need to do is assign the person to the role.

In other cases, where the organization is very large and people are committed to many projects, you will not know who is free. In this scenario you will need to draft your plan to see who you need and when. Then you will need to check resource availability before you can make an assignment. In certain organizations, you will also need to formally request resources for your project.

At the end of this step, you might also want to check the resource loading, so you can find and fix any over allocations due to the new work assignments you have just made.

B. Desk Check Project Plan

"If you would hit the mark, you must aim a little above it;
every arrow that flies feels the attraction of earth."

– Henry Wadsworth Longfellow (1807 - 1882), US poet and writer

By this stage, your project should be well planned. It is important to have a step where you stand back and review the plan thoroughly. Now that you have created lots of tasks and artifacts, you should look at the entire project in a Gantt (time sequenced) chart on in a Kanban chart (with buckets and cards). You will very likely see adjustments to make before the plan goes live.

It is also a good idea to have some of your colleagues peer review your plan.

The Time, Quality, Cost Trade-off

As part of your desk check, you and the team should be aware of the time–quality–cost triangle or trade-off discussed earlier in the handbook. These conflicting constraints are normal on a project and to be expected. You are trying to balance the scope that you need to deliver on the project with the time available to achieve the right level of quality for the cost and resources that you are allowed to spend on the project. At this point, you will want to make decisions on where to trade-off now or later as needs be. It is also a good idea to document these decisions and perhaps run those by your project sponsor if some of the trade-offs are significant. The key point is that thinking about the project in terms of time–quality–cost will likely lead to some revision of the planning you have done up to this point. This is positive, because it will protect your plan and make it better before you start into execution.

C. Notify Team of Responsibilities

It is all very well to plan a project in detail but you need to let team members know the plan for success. High quality communication increases the likelihood your plan for success will come true. Project team members are very smart and capable so be sure to empower them by letting them know what is going on. This is the essence of collaborative project management. Three mechanisms to manage and facilitate this communication include:

i. Involve your team on some or all of the prior planning steps.
ii. Host a project kick-off meeting to introduce team members to the project and walk them through the project site.
iii. Set up Automated Reminders
     - Enable your collaborative project site to automatically notify all new work assignments via email.
     - Set up the "My Work" report or dashboard on your collaborative project site.
     - Use scheduled emails with nudges for upcoming or late work. For example, early Monday mornings send an email of the work due for the week and then on Thursday morning send another email with work still open and due this week.

Questions for a "Project Planning" REP

Start: Apply some of this guidance to your current project, even if the project started, when you are ready or feel the need to REP this area.

Evolve: Use some of the guidance from this chapter that you think would be helpful, on your next project.

R
E
P
Journal

Stage 3 – Work the Project

Introduction

This chapter will guide you through the typical project team member experience on collaborative projects and will refer to:

- Team member commitment
- Team member process / rhythm
- Team member responsibilities.

> *"I love deadlines. I like the whooshing sound they make as they fly by."*
> – *Douglas Adams (1952-2001) English Humorist*

The Essence

Why do we need a stage "Work the Project"? Well, this is where the bulk of the project work takes place. This is where the actual project work occurs. You also need to be mindful that team members are extremely distractible, as you can see in the wonderful quote above from Douglas Adams.

What does this stage entail? In summary, you want to give the team members some direction on how to proceed, how to work on the project, and how to collaborate. This will enable the team members to step up to the plate and help you to manage the project collaboratively.

Time Out

A few questions for you to help you get your head into this chapter:

- How do you and the other team members work and collaborate on existing projects?
- How do you work together to deliver on the project objective?
- How do your team members approach their project work? What is their work rhythm?

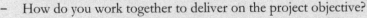

Team Member Commitment

Your project has now started and everybody (hopefully!) knows what he or she is meant to do. In a collaborative project, you are essentially asking the team members for three commitments as described here. You might even use these words in the three short paragraphs on this page below if you are very new to collaborative project management!

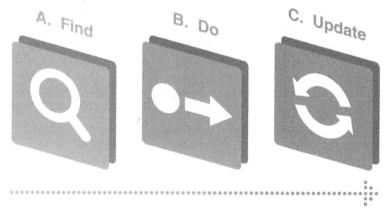

A. Find work

Using one of the many notifications (e.g. My Work report, automated emails, etc.), find your work so you know what you are committed to delivering for the project.

B. Do work

Naturally enough, go do the work! In many cases, the actual work products (e.g. a proposal or design) can be created and updated in the collaborative project site.

C. Update progress on work

Use the datasheets or forms provided in the collaborative site to record your progress on what is done or in progress, and use the project site to record any issues that need attention.

Team Member Process / Rhythm

It is very likely that the team members on your projects will be involved in more than one project and will have other work responsibilities. As such, they will find it difficult to keep up with all the deadlines. In fact, do not be surprised if some of the team members are so focused on the work, that they are not too worried about or focused on any of the project deadlines!

As the project manager, you will want to ensure that team members understand their responsibilities. Using the simple three-step explanation above (find work, do work, update work) is an easy way to communicate this expectation. Making this commitment clear is something you may wish to do at the project kick-off meeting. You will also want to give team members a weekly rhythm to follow, for example:

- *[Monday]* Review the latest plan and your personal commitments (via dashboards or automated emails)
- *[Everyday]* Do lots of work and make great progress!
- *[Late Thursday]* Make a progress update on your tasks and issues in the project site (if not already done)
- *[Friday at 10am]* Weekly team meeting for 30 minutes.

Team Member Responsibilities

It is a very positive and progressive step to talk to team members about the responsibility they are expected to carry on a collaborative project. In addition to the suggestions above, you can ask collaborative team members to have the courage to:

- Take responsibility given
- Contribute to the team
- Challenge the direction respectfully
- Accept the agreed team direction
- Participate in the speed of the project
- Always take positive actions.

The Four C's of an Ideal Team

The earlier chapter, 'Cultivate Your Leadership Approaches (Models and Practices)', offers lots of advice on selecting a team model for collaborative leadership. Repeated here from that earlier chapter is one suggestion for the ideal dynamics of a high performing team. You wish this atmosphere for your project team.

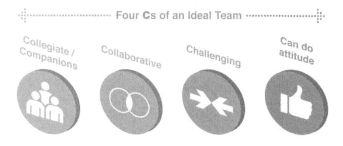

- **C**ollegiate / **C**ompanions (friendly and enjoyable with no need for fear)
- **C**ollaborative (on the one team and on the one project helping each other)
- **C**hallenging (to each other – but respectfully) with the **C**onflict required for innovation. Be comfortable asking and answering uncomfortable questions.
- **C**an do attitude – and no such thing as I/we can't.

Questions for a "Project Execution" REP

<u>Start</u>: Apply some of this guidance to your current project, even if the project has started, when you are ready or feel the need to REP this area.

<u>Evolve</u>: Use the guidance in this chapter on your next project. Or perhaps recommend it to some of your colleagues for their projects.

Stage 4 – Track and Re-Plan the Project

Introduction

This chapter will take you through the steps involved in collaboratively tracking and re-planning your project.

> *"There is nothing in this world constant, but inconstancy."*
> – Jonathan Swift (1667-1745), Irish poet, essayist and cleric

The Essence

Why do we need to track and re-plan the project? Remember the advice from the Prussian Army General when he said that no plan will ever survive the first encounter with the enemy?

What do we do in this fourth stage? We actively track and honestly re-plan the project with the team. It is quite difficult to do this sometimes, but it is that simple. This is what we need to do.

Time Out

At this stage, it would be good to ask yourself:

- How do you track and re-plan projects?
- Is this the way everyone else in your group tracks and re-plans projects, or are there other approaches in practice?

Track and Re-Plan the Project

As the team are working through their assignments, it is good to remember Murphy's Law: *"that which can go wrong, will go wrong!"* There are some project managers I know who claim Murphy was an optimist!

Some tasks may be ahead of schedule, but almost certainly, some are falling behind. One thing you can be sure of is that the project is not running exactly to the plan you started with. That is why it is called a plan! Allied to this, other unanticipated problems or issues may have emerged.

This fourth stage will help you understand three steps needed to track where the project is at, re-plan, and communicate the newly adjusted plan.

A. Check and understand the project's progress
B. Find and manage exceptions (e.g. issues, risks and change requests)
C. Re-plan the project.

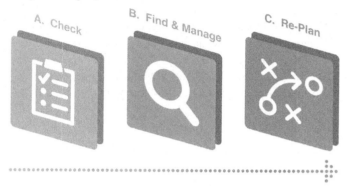

A. Check and Understand Project Progress

By fair means or foul, you need to figure where the project is before you can re-plan, or before you and the team re-plan together. You need to know which tasks are ahead of schedule and which tasks are falling behind. Below are three simple ways that you can get this information.

i. Virtual Check

This is "collaborative project management" so be careful not to waste time asking people for basic project information that they have entered into a collaborative project site. Rather than calling everyone for a status update, you should be able to examine the various (project, issue, work, resource) reports, notebooks, and conversations on the collaborative project site you set up.

If your team members are following the simple guidelines in Stage 3 of this guide ("Work the Project"), you will have plenty of project updates to review from the comfort of your own desk. A sample set of reports to review in any project site might be:

- Home page to get a quick project status
- Overdue work
- Work by assignee
- The full task list (in a Gantt or Kanban view)
- Resource utilization
- Issues
- Status of your own work!

ii. Individual Check

MBWA – 'Managing by Walking About' is one of the oldest forms of management. Walk about, phone about, and talk to the team members and customers to get their take on the project status. Remember – this is collaborative project management, so your team members will expect you to show up!

iii. Team Check

You do not want to have project meetings for the sake of meetings so you do need to be careful with how these meetings are managed. I hope that you found helpful ideas in the "Manage Meetings (Ten Suggestions)" chapter earlier in this handbook! Here is a sample five-point agenda that you as a new project manager might consider for your team meeting:

a) **Status** *and Health of the Project*

b) **Issues**: *Review, discuss and resolve (in so far as possible) any open issues*

   Project meetings can easily get derailed and run over time, so it is key to use the time to solve problems as a team. Not all issues will be resolved at the project meeting but discussing issues will open them for further deliberation.

c) **Next**: *Look at upcoming tasks*

   It is good to look at what is up next. It makes people aware and helps them focus on the essential upcoming work. While the team is together, it is a good time to get the varied inputs of team members on key tasks scheduled to start soon.

d) **Achieved**: *Look at tasks achieved recently or at least the milestones*

   Many project meetings over-run in my experience! You need to be a really organized and disciplined facilitator to have meetings start and finish on time. If you know that project meetings will over-run, you should not start the meeting with this item as team members will tend to enjoy talking about what was achieved last week, and this may eat most of the meeting time.

e) **Other** *Business*

While you need not follow this agenda, it is important to have some sort of standard agenda or meetings will not be energizing or effective. You want meetings to be both.

"There are only two qualities in the world: efficiency and inefficiency; and only two sorts of people: the efficient and the inefficient."

– George Bernard Shaw (1856-1950), Irish writer, dramatist and critic

B. Find and Manage Exceptions

You know where the project is at after this last step ('Check and understand the project's progress'), but do not start re-planning just yet! You should now check for outstanding exceptions. Exceptions on a project may come in many forms but issues, risks, and change requests are the most common.

You will want to resolve any open issues you can to remove roadblocks to the schedule. It could be that the issue's resolution changes your plan. Similarly, look at open risks and decide if you need a mitigation plan to reduce the likelihood of the risks transpiring. In some cases, what was once a risk is now a reality, and contingency steps are now necessary.

You may also need to process project change requests, which often means consulting with team members and possibly project sponsors to see what course they advise and authorize. Approving a change request can impact your project, so best to know this impact before you start the re-planning in earnest.

As a new project manager, it is important not to be afraid to make adjustments.

"Like all weak men he laid an exaggerated stress on not changing one's mind."

– William Somerset Maugham (1874-1965), English writer, dramatist and physician

C. Re-Plan the Project

Some project managers are natural re-planners and do this daily as the project progresses. Others are so busy, re-planning itself needs to be logged as a project task. Styles and personalities come into play here. Some people embrace change and love re-planning and some decidedly do not!

Here are three sub-steps you might consider for this re-plan step, whether you do it as necessary or at a set time every week:

   i. Re-assign Work and Send Notifications
  ii. Report to and Work with the Appropriate Stakeholders
 iii. Tailor the Project Site as Needed.

i. Re-assign Work and Send Notifications

By this stage, you have gathered enough information to re-plan the project. In reality, you were making some adjustments as you executed the preceding two steps, but you need to perform the remaining changes before you formally re-publish and re-communicate the plan.

a) Project Redefinition
The project is defined and laid out in a series of artifacts, e.g. project statement, tasks, issues, etc. Updating these can be as simple as traversing the lists in the project site and making adjustments.

b) Project Re-Assignments
If the structure or workloads of your project have changed, you will need to reassign work to different team members. At this stage, you should also find and fix any over assignments.

c) Notifications
Check that the changes are still going out through the notifications mechanisms set up earlier in "Stage 2 - Plan and Setup the Project".

ii. Report to and Work with the Appropriate Stakeholders

Now that the changes are made, you may need to update your stakeholders. Your project sponsor will need to know what changes are afoot. It is best that this news comes directly from you, the project manager. If the news is bad, do not be afraid to take this step. It is important. Working with your project sponsor may involve some of the following:

- Deliver periodic status reports (printed, emailed or verbal)
- Raise exceptions including project change requests, top issues and top risks
- Resolve sponsor level issues and apply the resolution through project re-planning (if appropriate).

iii. Tailor the Project Site

In "Stage 1 - Initiate the Project" you decided how best to manage the project. As the project progresses and naturally changes, you may have to change how you manage to match the evolving needs of the project. Maybe you opted not to manage risks very formally at the outset, but you now believe that the project is changing at a pace that is not healthy, so you now need to introduce more formalized risk management. Alternatively, perhaps you initially decided to manage with issues, risks, and change requests but now realize that this was too much project management for this project. In this case, you scale back the amount of project management you use.

As you periodically re-plan the project, you will do well as a project manager to ensure you have 'just the right' amount of management for the project in hand. At this stage of the process, you can tailor the project approach and site to mimic the desired amount of collaborative project management.

Questions for a "Project Re-Planning" REP

<u>Start</u>: Apply some of this guidance to your current project, when you are ready or feel the need to REP this area.

<u>Evolve</u>: Use the guidance in this chapter on your next project or perhaps even recommend it to some of your colleagues for their projects.

Stage 5 – Close the Project

Introduction

This chapter will guide you through how to benefit from an orderly close to the project with your team.

> *"There must be a beginning of any great matter, but the*
> *continuing unto the end until it be thoroughly finished yields*
> *the true glory."*
> *– Sir Francis Drake (1540-1596) English navigator*

The Essence

Why formally close the project? By definition, a project has a start and finish so it needs to be closed out. If you do not shut it down who will? In the immortal words of Francis Drake, this is where you get the glory! What do you do in this stage? You and your team will learn from the project as you close the project together.

Time Out

- How do you close projects? Or do you?
- Is this the way others in your group closes projects, or are other practices in play?

Close the Project

As stated earlier, we can depict project management as follows:

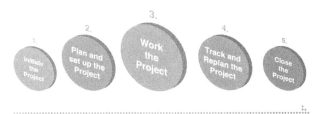

With this in mind, much of the project is about working the project, figuring what is happening, and periodically re-planning to ensure the end goals are met. Health warning! Project Management does require a determination to keep going to the end, as there will be difficult periods on most projects. The earlier sections 2 and 3 of this handbook include many suggestions relating to physical and mental wellbeing, and personal and situational leadership to help you overcome these challenges.

There comes a time when the project needs to be shut down. As we know, one of the hallmarks of a project is a defined start and a defined end. This is what marks a project out from processes and continuous operations. A set of steps for an orderly project close stage is as follows:

A. Close out the project site
B. Run project post-mortem and track lessons learned
C. Capture any useful modifications made to the project site for use on future projects.

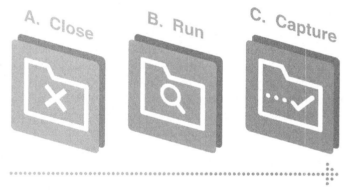

A. Close Out the Project Site

On an administrative note, you now have a live project site for a project that is just finished. At a minimum, you should mark the project closed so that anyone who visits the site can quickly see that the project is completed. You also want to ensure that the project does not appear in any current reports going to senior management. It is usually best not to fully archive and hide the site for a time. Normally when projects are completed, it is really hard to get any information about them after a few months. The half-life of project information is very short! It helps to look back at similar project sites when planning new projects.

B. Run Project Post-Mortem

No project ever goes perfectly. None! If you consider the approach advocated in this handbook, we have suggested that you have regular tracking and re-planning steps. This is essentially a tacit admission that we are learning as we go on every project, as indeed is the oft-recommended use of the "Start|Evolve" approach to collaborative project management.

If we can learn as we go, then why not learn as we finish? There is a tendency to take flight when the project is over and move to the next one. However, the more you learn from the project you have just completed, the more successful you will be with the project you are about to start.

Remember this handbook is written primarily for "accidental", "occasional" or new project managers. These project managers generally have no formal training and few experiences managing projects, so any learning opportunity should not be wasted! It is also important to remember that as a project manager, we have been a leader of the project, but not the sole owner of its processes and tasks. With this in mind, it is respectful to ask team members what they thought of the project. Many project managers say they do not have time to do project post-mortems. However, the same professionals seem to have time to fall into the same traps and then spend time fixing the issues. A stitch in time saves nine!

"It is a capital mistake to theorize before one has data."
– The Adventures of Sherlock Holmes (1892)

Very switched on project managers and team members will be keeping a list of items for the post mortem as the project progresses. It can be very helpful to host the post mortem in a different and relaxed setting – perhaps away from the office – or maybe in the office with some nice snacks served. This change of location can help the flow of feedback.

To do a good post-mortem it is helpful to have a set of open questions to ask. Questions naturally help the participants reflect on the project from various angles, so the quality of feedback and learning is best. A sample set of simple and open questions include:

– What went well on this project?

- What did not go so well on this project?
- What did we not do on this project that might have helped?
- What specific actions should we take to adjust the approach to the next project we do as a team?

Team members are very smart, so the real goal of this step is to give people the time and the space to reflect on the project. This step can be carried out simply enough once the time is set aside. A set of possible mechanisms include:

- Meeting: The team meets to talk through the project in a facilitated session.
- Survey: You give people a survey to complete.
- Meeting and Survey: You do a combination of both; people answer questions in advance and then attend a meeting to thoroughly discuss the survey answers and make some recommendations for future projects.

On larger projects, you can run a "Lessons Learned"/ "Review" exercise modelled on this post-mortem at the end of each project stage.

C. Capture Project Site Modifications

If the collaborative project site was modified as you went through the project, you will want to review the adaptations and apply those approved to the template for new project sites. This is a very pragmatic and efficient way to improve your approach to project management.

Questions for a "Project Close" REP

Start: Apply some of this guidance to your current project, even if the project has started, when you are ready or feel the need to REP this area.

Evolve: Use the guidance in this chapter on your next project, or perhaps, even recommend it to some of your colleagues for their projects.

Build your Own Approach

Now that you are this far through this Personal and Collaborative Leadership handbook, it could be helpful to reflect on how you might manage your projects. Below are three summaries of the stages and steps presented in the preceding chapters to help facilitate this process for you.

"Whatever good things we build end up building us."
– Jim Rohn (1930-2009) American entrepreneur, author and motivational speaker

Low Adoption

Perhaps you just use the five high level stages as your guide:
1. Initiate the Project
2. Plan and Setup the Project
3. Work the Project
4. Track and Re-Plan the Project
5. Close the Project.

Medium Adoption

Maybe you use the five high level stages and some of the three steps in each stage as your guide:
1. Initiate the Project
   A. Get the Project Approved, Sponsored, and Resourced
   B. Decide a Project Management Process
   C. Create a Collaborative Project Site
2. Plan and Setup the Project
   A. Plan the Project
   B. Desk Check the Project Plan
   C. Notify the Team of their Responsibilities
3. Work the Project
   A. Find Work
   B. Do Work
   C. Update Progress on Work (recording any issues)
4. Track and Re-Plan the Project
   A. Check and Understand the Project's Progress
   B. Find and Manage Exceptions (e.g. issues, risks)

      C. Re-Plan the Project
5. Close the Project
      A. Close Out the Project and the Project site
      B. Run Project Post-mortem and Track Lessons Learnt
      C. Capture any Useful Modifications (made to the project site for use on future projects).

High Adoption

You may wish to use the five high level stages, some of the three steps, and some of the associated sub-steps as your guide, when building your own process / approach:

1. Initiate the Project
      A. Get the Project Approved, Sponsored and Resourced
      B. Decide a Project Management Process
      C. Create a Collaborative Project Site
2. Plan and Setup the Project
      A. Plan the Project
          i. Complete the Project Statement
          ii. Define and Allocate Tasks
          iii. Add the other Project Artifacts Needed
          iv. Assign the Work
      B. Desk Check the Project Plan
          i. Work the Time-Quality-Cost Trade Off
      C. Notify the Team of their Responsibilities
          i. Host a Project Kick-Off Meeting
          ii. Enable your collaborative site with the facility to email notifications on all new work assignments
          iii. On your collaborative site, setup an easy to find "My Work" report / dashboard
          iv. Setup scheduled emails with nudges for upcoming or late work.
3. Work the Project
      A. Find Work
      B. Do Work
      C. Update Progress on Work (recording any issues)
4. Track and Re-Plan the Project
      A. Check and Understand the Project's Progress
          i. Virtual Check

          ii.   Individual Check

          iii. Team Check

    B. Find and Manage Exceptions (e.g. issues, risks)

    C. Re-Plan the Project

          i.   Re-assign Work and Send Notifications

          ii.   Report to and Work with the Appropriate Stakeholders

          iii. Tailor the Project Site (to match the evolving needs of the project)

5.   Close the Project

    A. Close Out the Project and the Project site

    B. Run Project Post-mortem and Track Lessons Learnt

    C. Capture any Useful Modifications (made to the project site for use on future projects).

Questions for a "Collaborative Project Management" REP

Start: I am not suggesting that you should follow every stage, step, and sub-step in sequence as presented in this handbook. However, if you are new to project management, you could walk through the stages presented in summary above, design your own collaborative project management approach using these guidelines as a starting point, and try it for real, when you are ready or feel the need to REP this area.

Evolve: Do this process design exercise for your next few projects, until you get a process and rhythm that you find helpful.

Collaborative Project Management Leadership

It goes without saying that leadership is required to successfully deliver an amazing project, but what does this mean in practice?

- **Personal Leadership** (reference Section 2 of this handbook): The entire project team, and especially the project manager, need to be at their best and will ideally bring their 'A game' to the project. The team need to be in a good place personally and this, while desirable on so many levels, does not happen by accident. This requires investment and personal management in areas such as energy, attitude, awareness, personality and time-management. As it happens, this level of personal leadership also develops the same practices and habits that lead to a happier and healthier personal life.

- **Situational Leadership** (reference Section 3 of this handbook): A project team encounters many common repeated situations, including various types of meetings, decisions, variable performance, awkward communications, unclear roles and responsibility lines, etc. It is helpful and important to have patterns, practices, and protocols to successfully manage these recurring situations.

- **Collaborative Project Management** (reference Section 4 of this handbook): The world is evolving to a place where more and more of our people want, deserve, and are being given project leadership responsibilities. In many cases this responsibility is not accompanied by line management authority, nor does it need to be. This ask or grant requires that each person have leadership approaches that they can call on, and that these approaches are adaptable and compatible with the requirements of collaborative project management. It is also important that the organization develops project and team models designed to accommodate and encourage these higher levels of leadership.

Process Management

Introduction

The prior chapters in this Section 4 focus on project management and more specifically on the process of collaborative project management. This last chapter in this section, in six pages, explores the nature of processes (starting in 1776!), and process improvement. Exploring process management is not for everyone, though I find it very interesting and relevant, but as with all chapters feel free to skip for now and come back later as you wish.

The Essence

A project is a temporary, one-off endeavor with specific objectives. A process can be defined as a series of repeated actions that produce something or lead to a particular repeatable result. Understanding the difference between a project and a process will help you to apply the right approach to upcoming work.

Definition of Process

In 1776, Adam Smith wrote "*An Inquiry into the Nature and Causes of the Wealth of Nations*", and as a result, the poor man is often blamed for creating modern day capitalism! Consider the following description from the first few pages in his book and ask yourself: is this a project or a process?

> "One man draws out the wire, another straights it, a third cuts it, a fourth points it, a fifth grinds it at the top for receiving the head: to make the head requires two or three distinct operations: to put it on is a particular business, to whiten the pins is another ... and the important business of making a pin is, in this manner, divided into about eighteen distinct operations, which in some manufactories are all performed by distinct hands, though in others the same man will sometime perform two or three of them."

As I'm sure you've guessed, the making of pins in this manner is definitely a process. However, the initial set up of the pin factory is a major project. Subsequent improvements or modifications to the factory might also be treated as projects.

Process Improvement Models

If you're serious about implementing and improving project management across a group, a knowledge of process improvement models can be very insightful and extremely helpful.

The Deming "PDSA" Model

W. Edwards Deming, an American quality expert, was brought to Japan in the aftermath of World War II to help in the reconstruction of the nation. Deming had been influenced by the Shewhart cycle from 1939 and brought what was later called the Deming wheel to Japan in 1950. The Deming wheel was depicted as PDCA (Plan, Do, Check, Action). Deming himself later changed the cycle to PDSA (Plan, Do, Study, Act). In later years the Plan, Do, Check, Act or Plan, Do, Study, Act cycles have been used as instruments of continuous improvement for processes. They have been famously associated with the Japanese quality assurance, total quality control, and continuous process improvement movements.

These simple but powerful cycles can be very helpful in improving project management in an organization. Think of it in the following generic and repeatable terms:

- Plan the process change you want to introduce
- Do or implement the process change
- Check or study the impacts of the change
- Act on this to make any adjustments that are appropriate.

And some time later start the cycle again, so the cycle of improvement continues. If a group uses PDSA properly, the group is systematically in a constant cycle of very positive continuous process improvement.

ISO 9000 Series

The ISO 9000 series can also be very powerful for process improvement. The essence of the ISO 9000 series is that you, in an intelligent way, decide what you're going to do and write this up as a set of policies, procedures, and standards. You then train everybody in the enactment of these approaches. And finally you continuously check how you're doing against that which you said you would do. These continuous checks include audits and associated corrective actions (arising from the audit findings). It's possible to use the ISO 9000 series either as a mechanism for improving quality internally and / or to get the quality of your process assured by an external agency, which would result in the award of an ISO 9000 certification for your process (but not your product).

The CMM – Capability Maturity Models

To round out this brief introduction to process improvement models, it's worth adding a short explanation of the Capability Maturity Model (CMM). This model came out of work facilitated at Carnegie Mellon University in the late 1980s. The work is sometimes much maligned because, as with all models, it can be abused by people who want to prove they are better than they really are. However, the essence of the model has some really excellent thinking.

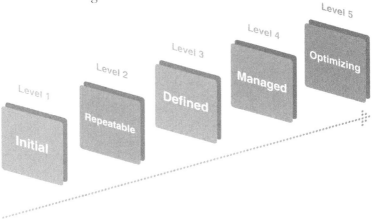

The model is essentially a five level model and any process can be at any one of these levels.

1. Initial: Level One is characterized by being chaotic or informal. You could say that all processes are at least at Level One!

2. Repeatable: To say that a process is repeatable means that it can work pretty much every time. However, it tends to be overly dependent on the heroics of a small number of people to make it so. If these people leave the organization, the process would more than likely fail to deliver the intended results.

3. Defined: At this level, there is a thought-out and documented step-by-step set of policies, processes, procedures, and work instructions, and ideally, tools to automate some of the steps. The idea is that new people can come and go and the process will guide whoever is involved in that particular process. Of course, there's an implicit assumption that people have to be trained and capable of executing the process, but the process is at least defined.

4. Managed: Here, the process has a high degree of management oversight, is instrumented, and measured. With these metrics, we know where we're at. We might not always like it, but we'll know how the process is performing.

5. Optimizing: Finally, Level Five, is called Optimizing. Note that it's not called optimized as this would indicate an end point. Processes are dynamic, and as such, we need to tweak and optimize them from time to time. The practice here is to use the metrics and other information to make decisions to implement as process changes. In earlier levels, we have basic checks in place and we make changes because we think or believe they make sense. But at Level Five, metrics and data are also guiding us intelligently to make changes.

Can you see how this CMM might apply to the process of project management in your organization? Maybe you can decide what level your project management process is at. Is it Level One, Two, Three, Four or is it at Level Five? Identifying this current level of project management will help you decide what investment comes next on your collaborative project management journey.

REP versus PDSA, ISO 9000, CMM

In Section 1 REP was presented as a personal change management process. This chapter presented PDCA, PDSA, ISO 9000, and CMM as organizational process improvement models. I am sure you can see the overlaps and similarity of thinking.

Time Out

This might be a good time to take a time out and to think through some of the ideas presented in this chapter. The following questions may well be worth asking and answering for yourself:

- What are some of the examples of critical processes that you have in your group?
- Do some of these processes need definition, improvement, or both?
- Do you have a process for project management or some aspects of project management? Do you have a process defined for collaborative project management?
- Based on your thinking, what are the next actions necessary for you and / or your group on the process management or process improvement front, especially as it relates to collaborative project management?

Section 5. Going Further

Facilitate a Group Training Course

I was asked to run a course at work based on this handbook. It was not a request I was expecting, but of course it made sense, once the request came through.

I am pretty sure that the expectation was that I would give a series of traditional classes with me as the 'expert'. The latter did not feel right, as personal and professional change with REP is all about making your own decisions based on your own research and then moving these ideas and decisions into execution, and later reflecting on how these experiences flowed or did not.

REP implies a lot more personal responsibility for learning, rather than expecting to be taught, which is what a lot of us have become accustomed to at school. This method of teaching by instruction has not always served us well in later life. As I prepared to facilitate this course, I was reminded of the current shift in education to the 'flipped class', where students are given materials by their teachers to teach themselves alone and in peer groups, and then the teachers help with the difficult parts of the homework. Imagine this, you teach yourself and the teacher helps you with your homework! This allows students to learn at a time, pace and place they are more comfortable with. Imagine how difficult it is for a teacher to bring thirty students of mixed ability and different concentration levels along at the same time and pace. I have a new respect for my teachers from school and university as I think of this challenge! The 'flipped class' is a reversal of the traditional classroom experience. The preceding few sentences do not do justice to the very successful changes happening in some of the most innovative schools around the world, but hopefully you get the basic idea.

I gladly accepted the challenge to facilitate (not deliver!) a course based on this handbook, and decided to use the 'flipped class' approach, and it worked well. The pages in 'Appendix 1: Outline of the Training Course' will explain how we together experienced and ran the course using this handbook, so that you can do something similar if you see the need and the benefit.

REP to New Habits

So, where to next? The leadership practices in Sections 2, 3, and 4 of this handbook touch on the areas of physical health, mental health, spiritual wellbeing, intellectual alertness, professional and work enrichment. I know from personal experience that these and similar practices can be of great help.

Be Intentional about REP

It is no accident that this handbook starts and finishes with REP. Success in the practices of personal and collaborative project management and leadership, as described in this handbook, do require a focused investment. This success will not come by accident, but is extremely achievable with the right approach. Allied to this we all need our organizations, and that means our people, to grow to better manage the challenges we face today, and also to be ready to manage the unimagined challenges of the future. At the same time everyone is very busy with the day job, so this much needed growth tends to be taken for granted or in some cases ignored.

REP – a Summary

The REP protocol (described in Section 1 of this handbook and summarized again here) presents a process comprised of three very simple but trusted practices to help individuals and thus organizations grow in a gradual but sure manner. REP stands for **R**esearch, **E**xecute, and **P**ost-Mortem and is a play on the word 'repetition'. Repetition is, of course, an important aspect of mastery. As a recap (because we know that repetition is helpful!):

- **Research**: This first phase is spent seeking out and learning new practices, skills and ideas. This phase should be a fun exploration. Any interesting findings are logged in a REP Journal. The Research phase ends by selecting a subset of the practices to try.
- **Execute**: This second phase is where time is allocated to experiment with these new ideas, to try them for real. The Execute phase is necessary to see if and how the practices can be adopted to your context. It is in this doing that much of the

real learning takes place.

- **Post-Mortem**: This third phase allows the time and space to reflect on the outcomes of the new practices. This reflection requires a time out, however short. The end result of the Post-Mortem may likely be a commitment to REP, again straight away or at some later date, to add more practices or to sharpen existing ones.

REP is designed to be repeated any time new skills, habits, practices are desired. In summary, REP is a very simple, efficient, and effective personal change management process.

Enjoy the Journey with REP

Quite honestly there are too many leadership practices in this handbook for one person to successfully take into daily or weekly habit in one sitting. I hope you see this as a real positive. So please let yourself off the hook!

The trick is not to rush, but to gradually adopt the new practices that appeal to you. REP, as described in Section 1 of this handbook, will lead to higher levels of success, capability, creativity and mastery for yourself and also for your teams. If you set time aside and you commit to REP each week and try out or recommit to just one new practice or idea each week, imagine where you will be after a few months or a year. Enjoy the journey!

Appendix 1: Outline of the Training Course

Course Outline

As explained above, and as you will see in the following pages, this was not a traditional course. However, the participants called it a course and that designation felt good for people, so I was happy to label this series of workshops as a course. I advertised the course with the following modules (derived from this handbook):

1. Course Introduction
2. Manage Your Energy
3. Have a Healthy and Positive Attitude
4. Better Manage Your Time - Part 1
5. Better Manage Your Time - Part 2
6. Know and Leverage Your Personality
7. Make Good Decisions
8. Have Better Meetings
9. Cultivate Your Leadership and Teamwork Approaches
10. Deliver Effective Presentations
11. Know how to Manage Projects
12. Course Review and Look Forward

You could of course have more or less modules and order them in any way you wish, in your own delivery of such a course.

Introductory Session

I asked the participants to read the pages of the handbook on "Personal Change and REP" before coming to the introductory session. This was important background material, but it also set the expectation, that the participants were going to lead their own learning, education and change. In the opening session, which lasted about an hour, this was my outline, my "class plan" (with apologies to real teachers!):

Opening Remarks
  - Nora McGuinness … "*no such thing as you can't*"

- Éamonn McGuinness ... *"you can do anything you want to do in life, you just have to want to do it"* (If you get nothing from this Leadership course, but this, you are ahead already!)

Introduction and Intent:
- Very welcome and thanks for signing up!
- This course is first for you, and then for the others in the room. I really hope it makes a difference to and for you
- You can get lots of real benefit from this course, if you invest the time and effort
- I intend to do the course with you, as a student as well as a facilitator
- Explanation of the flipped class
- One rule/protocol: What is said in this room, stays in this room (only exceptions - if the person raises it with you outside the room).

"Personal Change and REP" Materials
- What Questions or Clarifications do you have?
- What Observations do you have on the ideas of REP and REP Journal?

What are your hopes for this course?
- but only if you wish to say in class
- feel free to email me these and other ideas afterwards

Your Homework!
- Read the chapter on "Manage Your Energy"
- Take note of questions and observations and bring them to the next class
- Mark with an * items you'd like to try out in your REP
- Start REP'ing

Close
- Any final questions or observations?
- Good luck!

In facilitating this session and all subsequent sessions, it was very important to make people feel at ease and ensure that everyone got to speak and engage. When questions were asked, I opened the question to the room, rather than jump in and answer it myself. In this way, the group was teaching the group and I was careful to augment or summarise the answers to the question. The sessions were round-table and highly participative. In each session participants had questions but they also had answers. It was important to help participants realise that they had answers. It was vital to leave class knowing for sure that this was not beyond them at all, as long as they made the commitment, as long as they accepted the responsibility.

First Module

As we exited the introductory session the participants left with their homework/research (as indicated in the "class plan" above). They had materials to teach themselves at a time, pace and place that worked for each of them. When we came back for the first actual session, here is the outline of the workshop that I had prepared and then facilitated:

Opening Remarks
- Welcome back - not sure everyone would come back!
- Reminder of our one rule/protocol ... Las Vegas rules strictly apply ... *"What is said in this room, stays in this room, with only one exception - if the person who raised the item brings it to you."* (p.s. - this includes me!)

Today's Session
- Let's now have a group discussion using Questions-Clarifications and/or Observations on the "Manage Your Energy" materials for this session
  - What Questions or Clarifications do you have?
  - What Observations do you have?
- Feel free (but no obligation) to comment on these two questions?
  - Is REP working for you yet?
  - Is the REP Journal idea working for you yet?

Your Homework!
- Read "Sharpen Your Attitude to Life"
- Take note of questions and observations and bring them

to the next class
- Mark with an * items you'd like to try out in your REP
- Keep REP'ing

Closing Remarks
- Reminder of our one rule/protocol ... Las Vegas rules apply ... "*What is said in this room, stays in this room, with only one exception - if the person who raised the item brings it to you.*"
- And remember ... "*you can do anything you want to do in life, you just have to want to do it.*"

One objective of each session was to ensure the research stage of REP was well under way, that each person had lots of ideas on the topic in questions (in the above case, "Manage Your Energy"), and that each person was reminded and ready to keep the REP moving through the execution and post-mortem phases.

Other Modules

Each of the following sessions followed the same pattern, as outlined in the 'First Module' above. We would tease out the area in question, and we would check in on how people were getting on with REP. Here is one more example of a session outline.

Opening Remarks
- Reminder of our one rule/protocol ... Las Vegas rules apply ... "*What is said in this room, stays in this room, with only one exception - if the person who raised the item brings it to you.*"

Today's Session
- Part 1: Let's have a group discussion using Questions and Observations on the "Sharpen Your Attitude to Life" materials you read for this session

- Part 2: Watch a video on and then talk about "Everyday Leadership" (using a TED talk)

- Part 3: Feel free (but no obligation) to comment on these two questions?
    - Your experience of REP thus far?

- The role of the Journal in your REP?

Your Homework!
- Read "Manage Your Time - A Five Step Approach"
- Take note of questions and observations and bring them to the next class
- Mark with an * items you'd like to try out in your REP
- Keep REP'ing

Closing Remarks
- Reminder of our one rule/protocol ... Las Vegas rules apply ... "*What is said in this room, stays in this room, with only one exception - if the person who raised the item brings it to you.*" (p.s. - this includes me!)
- And remember ... "*you can do anything you want to do in life, you just have to want to do it.*"

Closing Module

We ran the course over an eight month period with a workshop/ module about every three weeks. Each workshop lasted about two hours and explored an area of leadership from the handbook and also checked in on REP. Then we came to the final session, and the following was the outline used to guide the last workshop of the course.

Opening Remarks
- Reminder of our one rule/protocol ... Las Vegas rules apply ... "*What is said in this room, stays in this room, with only one exception - if the person who raised the item brings it to you.*"

Today's Session
- Explain today's Agenda

- What was your one main take-away from the course / group / handbook (that you are willing to share)?
  - Take a few minutes - and write at least one down.
  - Share please
  - My suggestion for my main take-away - is to "REP" (No surprises with my choice!)

- Let's watch this TED Talk from Carol Dweck: "*Growth Mindset - The Power of Believing You Can Improve*" – the video is 10 minutes – but watch especially from 5mins 40 secs
  - As we watch the video, pretend you are the student
  - https://www.ted.com/talks/carol_dweck_the_pow er_of_believing_that_you_can_improve

Follow Up
- Please give me KARA feedback (Keep; Adjust; Remove; Add) for both this course and also the handbook sometime in the next two weeks

Closing Remarks
- Again, thanks for your honest and generous participation.
- Remember ... "*you can do anything you want to do in life, you just have to want to do it.*"

Course Materials and Fees

There are no fees charged to use these materials to run your own course. These materials are provided by way of the gift economy. In lieu of fees, instructors and/or participants are asked to make a donation to the Jesuit Refugee Service (JRS) on https://jrs.net/ and please mention "Lead Inside Out" in your donation. I am sure your donation will be commensurate with the value received from the course and with what you can afford. Please be as generous as you can, as JRS is a very worthy cause. As is explained above, the course uses this handbook as the course materials for students. The handbook is available for purchase on Amazon. The entire proceeds of all book sales (and not just the profits) also go to the JRS.

About the Author

Éamonn McGuinness is the founder and CEO of two companies in the tech space. The customers of these companies, Amazon and Microsoft to name but two, are successful organizations in different sectors in many countries that Éamonn really enjoys working with. Éamonn is also fortunate enough to work with two amazing international not-for-profit organizations, one in an executive capacity and the other in a governance/advisory role. Éamonn also serves on two education boards, one national and the other international. All of these wonderful organizations are places of deep every-day learning for Éamonn.

Prior to this Éamonn worked with Digital Equipment Corporation, the United Nations and the Irish Army. He received his MSc in Computer Applications from Dublin City University and his undergraduate degree in Mechanical Engineering from the National University of Ireland Galway. Éamonn's first formal leadership training was in the Army Officer Cadet School, a very unique and privileged experience. Éamonn's good start in life is down to the schools he attended and the West of Ireland McGuinness and Cassidy families he was very lucky to be born into.

45455759R00126

Made in the USA
Middletown, DE
20 May 2019